❖

Cheaters

❖

Cheaters

180 Telltale Signs Mates are Cheating and How to Catch Them

Raymond B. Green
with psychological input by Marcella Bakur Weiner,
Ph.D., Ed.D.

New Horizon Press
Far Hills, New Jersey

Raymond B. Green
    Cheaters: 180 Telltale Signs Mates are Cheating and How to Catch Them

Cover Design: Robert Aulicino
Interior Design: Susan M. Sanderson

Library of Congress Control Number: 2002103023
ISBN: 0-88282-225-X
New Horizon Press

Manufactured in the U.S.A.

2007   2006   2005   2004   2003   /   5   4   3   2   1

DEDICATION

This book is dedicated to the three most precious gifts with which God has blessed me...

Britney, R. Shelby and Bryden

and to my soul mate and best friend,
Renatta

and her children, Tereska, Carleigh and Shanyssa

"Family is the treasures of my life."

"It will not matter what kind of car I drove, what kind of house I lived in or how much money I had in my bank account. It till not matter what my clothes looked like. However, one hundred years from now the world may be a little better because I was important in the lives of my children."

"Success is to be measured not so much by the position that one has reached in life as by the obstacles that one has overcome while trying to succeed."

Booker T. Washington (1856 – 1915)

Author's Note

The author and publisher disclaim any personal or property liability or expenses resulting directly or indirectly from the use of the equipment, techniques or strategies suggested in this book, as they are solely for educational and informational purposes only.

The author makes no assurance that the information contained in this book is comprehensive, nor does the author guarantee that the content matter will be suited to the particular needs of the reader. The information contained in this book is the opinion of the author. Furthermore, any psychological advice offered in this book should be considered a supplement to, not a replacement for, a thorough psychological exam and necessary counseling/treatment by a licensed health care professional.

The laws in your area may vary; therefore, you should seek independent, professional advice from a competent expert for your legal or family counseling matters. Check with a lawyer or your local police concerning the laws in your area regarding any methods described in this publication.

In order to protect privacy, fictitious names and identities have been given to all individuals in this book and otherwise identifying characteristics have been altered. For the purposes of simplifying usage, the pronouns his and her are often used interchangeably.

Table of Contents

FOREWORD

Not unlike Martin Luther and the posting of his ninety-three theses on the gates of the Cathedral of Wittenberg, Raymond B. Green of Brelen Investigations, Inc. posts his own how-to theses to help men and women who suspect a spouse/lover of having an affair. He is committed to the idea that marriage and other committed, monogamous relationships contain a premise as well as a promise: that the partners will not betray each other. When this premise is broken, the very foundation of the marriage, the sense of trust, is shaken, often irrevocably.

Green writes with a messianic zeal tempered by his many years as a private investigator. Writing with verve, clarity and objectivity about the men and women whose anguish over the possibility of discovering an affair is acute, unlike others, he is not dispassionate. Caring, love and compassion is felt in every word. Meticulously laying out before us the ins and outs of an affair, why it happens, when and how it takes place and the signs you can see if you remove your blinders, he teaches us what to do about this situation. With ease and the utmost skill, he gently takes the reader by the hand, choreographing your every move and alerting you to the tools you will need. Outlining some basic personality styles, Raymond Green helps you understand the differences between the men and women who choose to have affairs. A crucial key seems to be changes in attitudes, behaviors and activities. Focused as with a microscope, he points out that once a partner changes his or her routine code of behavior, that may be the beginning sign of an affair. Sensitizing you to this, he points the finger at precisely what to look for, holding up the mirror to reveal what is self-evident.

As Investigator Green suggests, men and women facing their mates' affairs behave differently. Research shows that women, suspecting their husbands of affairs, will turn to a confidante, usually another woman. Men, though not as widely, also often turn to a woman friend when suspicious of their wives. While this may be of some help, it also leads to a flood of opinions and advice that rarely soothes. Or, if it does, the relief is momentary until the pain of the betrayal strikes once again. At this crisis, while the primary need for the one betrayed is to be heard and understood, the person may become confused by and even resentful of an over-abundance of viewpoints.

Though many books have been written on marriage, few address the issue of the discovered affair and even fewer, actually none that I know of, of the suspected affair. In *Cheaters*, the path is laid out for you to take charge and do something about your life. This would include conscious, reality-oriented choices as to whether to stay and work it out or leave the marriage/relationship. First and foremost, however, you need the hard facts. This book will show you how to get them.

As a clinical psychologist for three decades who has listened to the heartbreak of those who tell me of their suspicions but lack confirmation, this book is a true gift. In simple, readable terms it spoon-feeds the reader, providing detailed how-to knowledge with tender loving care, a most rare combination.

I will place this book prominently on my bookshelf and share it not only with my colleagues and friends but also with my own clients, when appropriate. Insightful and workable, it can repair hearts and open up choices for all men and women who now have a reliable, trustworthy friend in this invaluable guide. I shall recommend it highly wherever I go.

Marcella Bakur Weiner, Ph.D., Ed.D.
Fellow, American Psychological Association
Professor (Adj.), Marymount Manhattan College

ACKNOWLEDGEMENTS

I would like to extend my heartfelt thanks to all those who supported me at the most difficult time in my life. Without them, this book would never have been possible!

You all know who you are...

Thank you, Renatta. Mere words cannot express the love I feel for you deep in my heart. Your love, laughter, beauty, compassion, confidence, support and guidance make up all the things I love about you. I thank God everyday that you are in my life. And the joy of having the girls in my life has added to the meaning of family. Let all our joys and challenges be learning experiences for bigger and better things.

A special thank you goes out to my family and close friends during that difficult time...

My children, Britney, Shelby and Bryden; my parents, Harold and Rita Green; Joseph and Janice Green-Gravel and family (Tony and Shelly, Kirby, Lorne, Michael, Gail); Frank and Suzanne Green and family (Kelly, Curtis and Andrew); Sharon and Scott Armstrong and family (Taylor, Ryan and Meghan); John and Susan Eisner and family (Jonathan, Elliot and David); Gordon Bouzane; Gary and Brenda Connell and family; Richard and Cheryl Luck and family; Gary and Debbie Fournier and family; Peter (Skip) and Kathy Rodgerson; Sarina McKinnon; Michael Haley; Adelaide Rodgerson and family; Terry and Ginger Wilson; Krista Kelly; Ann and Danny Murphy; Peggy and Jimmy Durning; Tommy Durning; Dave Booker; Bruce and Nancy Connell; Brad Lisson; Todd and Dafna Trites; Fraser and Heather Pride; Larry Hachey; Blake Broderson; Greg Jennings; Stephen McLaughlin; Terry Holt; and Robert Vey.

Introduction

In many ways this book is unique, because it does not try to mend or heal love relationships as the majority of relationship self-help books do. Reading this book probably won't save your marriage or relationship, although if it does then I'm truly happy for you. What I have set out to do, however, is to help those of you who suspect your mate is cheating to uncover the truth.

Perhaps you have noticed a few subtle signs of infidelity in your loved one, but you just can't be sure if you're overreacting or imagining things. Possibly the signs of cheating are more obvious, but you're deep in denial. Over time and through experience I have learned that if you have a gut feeling that your mate is cheating, then he or she probably is.

The saying "Love is blind" often describes the behavior of the people whose mates are unfaithful. Think about couples you know who have split up because of the infidelity of one of the partners. Who is always the last to know? Isn't it frequently true that many others know about the affairs except for the individuals who have been betrayed?

There are few things worse than suspecting your mate is cheating but not knowing if your suspicions are correct. The mental pain, the heartache and the emotional disarray can be overwhelming.

Unfortunately, cheating seems to be part of human nature and often a part of marital and romantic relationships. I've come to understand, however, that the majority of men and women instinctively know when something is wrong in their relationships and that somehow their mates have changed or are behaving differently. The problem is compounded when people refuse to believe what is happening, push it into a far corner of their mind and deny what their intuition is telling them.

As a private investigator and a man, I have had a tremendous amount of professional and personal experience dealing with unfaithful mates. I've discovered that I am no exception to the emotional blindness and denial of gut instincts when involved with a cheating mate.

This book is based on my professional skills as a former police officer and my years as a private investigator tracking cheating mates. The information I want to share with you was gleaned from countless hours of surveillance, interviews and observations. I want you to learn the signs of deception, the ways in which people cheat and the reasons why. As I desire for my clients, I want you to be able to confirm—or deny—your suspicions and gain peace of mind.

I believe true, faithful love relationships are worth working at and fighting for. However, they must be rooted in honesty and trust. If you have suspicions about your mate, you must learn all you can so you can either put those suspicions to rest or act upon the information you have learned. In this book I will teach you how to collect the information and gain the knowledge so important to the future of your relationship. Once you have the knowledge, you have the ability—the power—to make changes and chart your own course for the future.

chapter one

❖

He Said/She Said

Cheating by a mate or romantic partner is one of the most painful events a person can experience. It's not just learning about the illicit sexual encounter that is devastating. There is also the shock, rage and long-term hurt over the partner's deceit.

The emotions that victims experience include feelings of rejection, jealousy, humiliation, confusion, depression, anger and blame. When anger peaks, common sense and self-control are temporarily lost and a person can swing from self-pity to murderous thoughts and back again.

I'm frequently asked who cheats more—men or women? My answer is always the same: It's unimportant and irrelevant which gender cheats more. What is important is the fact that people are going to get hurt and their relationships will either end or be changed forever.

"Do cheaters have better sex?" is another question I'm often asked. My experience and research indicates that at the beginning of a clandestine relationship an individual usually does have better sex. However, as time goes by, the same problems or conflicts in the original relationship seem to crop up in the new one.

Research done by the Kinsey Institute, which is regarded by experts as the most credible source of information available about sex, shows that almost 90 percent of people with cheating mates know that their mates have betrayed them. Also, 78 percent of couples in which a partner has cheated and who stay together and try to work out their problems later describe their relationship as "unhappy" or "empty."

Throughout the book, we will examine the relationships of three couples who have experienced cheating mates. The couples, Mary and Dave, Ben and Julie and Liam and Wendy, are different in many ways but alike in one significant respect: Infidelity altered their lives forever.

Married for five years, Mary, twenty-seven, worked at a local hospital. Her husband Dave, twenty-nine, had a responsible position within their city's government. They both worked crazy hours and the shifts they worked—Mary arrived home as Dave was heading off to work—were as different as their goals. Mary was committed to her ever more demanding job, while Dave dreamt about moving out of their one-bedroom apartment into a house and having children.

Ben and Julie, both of whom had been previously married and divorced, were living together for about three years. Julie, a part-time retail clerk, has an eight-year-old daughter, Brittany, who lived with her in the house Ben, a contractor, had built after he had left his wife of seven years. Ben saw his two children from that marriage every second weekend and on some weekdays. Julie and Ben got along well despite Ben's heavy work schedule. He frequently was away from home even when his children were visiting, which displeased Julie. Ben was a good provider, and he assured Julie that hard work was necessary if they were to enjoy the "good life."

Another couple enjoying a prosperous life was Liam and Wendy, married for ten years and the proud parents of Brian, age five, and Shannon, age seven. Liam ran his own business and

Wendy was a homemaker. They owned a beautiful home and expensive cars. Liam worked hard and provided Wendy with everything she needed—or so he thought. The fact that they hadn't slept together for several years did not seem to bother Liam; he loved his wife and assumed she felt the same way about him. When confronted with evidence that pointed to Wendy's infidelity, Liam found it difficult to believe—especially when Wendy vigorously denied cheating.

As these stories will show, infidelity is an all-too-common occurrence. People make reckless decisions that adversely affect their mates, their children and themselves.

Some thoughts from Dr. Weiner:

Let's discuss some personality styles of cheaters before continuing. Not unlike the Greek myth in which Aphrodite sprang from the forehead of Zeus full-grown, cheating mates come into this world with their own personality traits. These characteristics, now recognized to be innate, may be those more likely to come under the influences of an affair than others. Along with this, there are gender differences which influence the reasons why and how people become cheating mates. We will examine some of these now.

Using Raymond Green's story of Wendy and Liam as an example, note that Wendy vociferously denied her affair even when confronted with evidence of it. She is the kind of woman who can easily detach; She is an example of the **Detached** type. Detachment is usually considered more of a male quality, however, some women can only attach themselves on an emotional level for short periods of time. These women live on the surface of their emotions. Nothing deep goes in. Nothing deep comes out. Wendy deprived her husband Liam of a consistent sex life, but ran to her lover whenever she could. Chances are if her lover pressed her for commitment, she would also flee from him. Her children and the consequences to them were also not considered by Wendy. For her, gratification of the moment was all that counted. Her style was: "I want it; I got it; I run with it." There were few lasting connections for Wendy. Why? No doubt if we examined her early experiences, they would provide some clues.

For Wendy, parenting probably was spotty at best. No one really counted or took responsibility for her. Whoever took care of her came and went; he or she was unreliable. With such deficient parenting, Wendy never developed the capacity to gather into herself an interior album, all the memories, thoughts, feelings, desires and wants we collect and cherish all through our lives. These things form the very basis of who we are. To Wendy, her growing up years were like an instant photo and whoosh—it faded and was gone forever.

As an adult, whenever she met a man more attractive or sexier than her husband, he became the man-of-the-moment with whom she could fall in love as easily as she could opt out of her committed relationship—her marriage. And so, she remained who and what she was—a supremely detached person. She perceived becoming emotionally involved as dangerous—and she had had little practice. Even sex with her husband, as Liam states, was out of the question. He attributed it to her not caring for him as much as he cared for her, but this kind of thinking was his version of wearing blinders. The truth is that sex with him was not exciting for her because its foundation was commitment, the attachment that comes with marriage. It was not Liam who was intolerable to Wendy. Rather, it was marriage itself that she found repugnant.

Marriage involves a total giving of one's self and Wendy didn't have a self to give. Her self consisted of disparate pieces that needed to fly, at the moment of impulse, from man to man.

Another personality type of cheater, usually more common among men, is the *Egoist*. His libido runs high. Sexual energy is his priority and he frequently resorts to the old cliché, "We (men) can't help it. It's all in our genes." He might complain about the lack of his wife's sexual interest, her gaining weight, her nagging or a boring sex life. Any woman he is attracted to he considers fair game. Whether a one-night stand or a long-term involvement, it is the excitement of the affair which is the ultimate turn-on. He cherishes novelty. Like a child who plays with a toy for a few minutes and then discards it to find one that is different, the egoist is always in pursuit of someone new.

Not one to be introspective, his gaze is usually outward bound. And if caught, accused or suspected, he rationalizes and points the finger at his mate: She has no time since the baby came; she is becoming too heavy and not dressing up like she used to; she gives too much time to her parents; she doesn't complement him like she did when they first met and on and on. The key here is that he comes first, now and always, regardless of the situation. Full of himself, he is the king of the castle. No questions asked. For him, affairs provide what he wants: the quiet of someone's home or a hotel room away from the pressures of daily life. And, most importantly, where he has his lover's full, undivided, adoring attention. This is what he truly craves.

How did he get to be this way? There are two possibilities: One is that he was neglected and ignored as a child; the other is that his parents gave him too much, too soon. For with love there needs to be limitations. These limitations must also be appropriate for the developmental stage of each child. A two-year old needs one thing; a child of twelve, another, and so on through life. Over-adoration makes the child feel that this is his birthright and that everyone he encounters will or should treat him the way his parents did.

Greg was one such egoist. The only boy in a family of six children, his parents doted on this youngest child who came to them in their later years. He was treated like royalty with every wish and whim catered to so that there were no frustrations or disappointments in his life. Yet, such things are limitations that we all need in order to socialize and mature.

With no obstacles to overcome, we are infantilized, never to find our strength and reach our maturity. Greg's parents treated him at sixteen and twenty-six the same way they treated him when he was a toddler. The world was his for the asking, he thought, and he asked for plenty.

When he married and he and his wife had their first child, she could no longer focus on him as she had before the baby arrived. Greg felt neglected. Did he not come before the baby? Could his meals/clothes/needs not be primary? Obviously, he was not the center focus in her life. And so his path of finding other women began. Better to be in a hotel or her place, than home. There, with no one but the two of them, he was once again king. No distractions. His lover of the moment would dress for him, eagerly await his entrance, embrace him with fervor, give sex without restrictions and hang on his every word. When this dynamic would falter, as it does when relationships become more familiar and routine, Greg once again would set out on his search for a new lover.

His wife began to suspect, but lacking the tools she needed to acquire evidence and busy with the child, she did not follow through and check on her suspicions. And so the marriage, now one in name only, continued but the sacred vows were cast aside.

A different type of cheater is the male who was sexually abused as a child, as was my client Rudy. Of importance is the identity of the abuser. If it was an older woman or a female relative, chances are the damage is accepted as being benign. Research states that the boy often sees this as his introduction to sexual experience.

If the abuser was a man, however, the damage may be severe. For it arouses fear in the victim: Did he really want it to happen and does that make him a co-conspirator to the abuse? Is he less of a man now? If he feels this way, as Rudy did, that his masculinity has been impaired, it is possible that he will need to define his prowess as a "real" man by the constant seduction of women. Such men may try to change the past and, instead of focusing on their marriages and bringing their fears/doubts/anxieties to their wives in order to receive nurturing and assurance, they turn elsewhere. And their marriages? They suffer and may be lost forever.

What can we conclude from this brief glimpse into the genesis of some people's cheating behavior? It seems that some individuals, in their attempts to fulfill spoken and unspoken needs that began in their childhoods, are disposed to infidelity. This doesn't mean that cheating on their mates is inevitable for them, simply that they may be at risk for such behavior.

What also becomes apparent as we read these thumbnail sketches of Wendy and Liam, Greg and Rudy is the damage that one partner's infidelity inflicts on a marriage or long-term relationship. While Wendy and Liam's marriage ended, both Greg's and Rudy's marriages continued in name only. Cheating is dangerous and destructive for all involved.

chapter two

❖

Why and How
Cheating Occurs

You have watched stories of betrayal and infidelity on television soap operas, seen them in movies, read about them in books and magazines and possibly heard about cheaters and cheating among friends and family. But it's always somebody else's tale. Having an unfaithful partner is like being in an airplane crash, getting a life-threatening disease or being struck by lightening. It's supposed to happen to somebody else, not you!

Usually, people don't wake up one morning and decide that today is the day they are going to hop into bed with someone new and be untrue to their mates. More likely, the idea of cheating has been channeling in and out of their minds for a period of time before they actually act. What is believed by experts and confirmed by my experiences is this: *When two people are in a long-term relationship, a partner is more likely to cheat than end the relationship.*

This fact is borne out by the experiences of our couples, Mary and Dave, Julie and Ben, and Wendy and Liam. In all three cases, the cheating partner did not want to leave or divorce his or her mate, despite the desire for a sexual adventure.

Mary and Dave worked different shifts and frequently seemed like strangers passing in the night—one coming home as the other was heading out to work. When Dave wasn't working, he was either playing hockey, immersed in a card game at a friend's house or sitting in front of the television. When Mary wasn't working, she was visiting her mother or a neighbor or enjoying a bingo game with her sister.

Mary had many friends, including Steve, whom Dave had met a few times. Steve even tagged along once when they went out together as a couple. It was fine by Dave. He trusted Mary. After all, Steve had been a friend of Mary's long before Dave had met her.

Dave and Mary were arguing a lot, though their friends thought they were getting along fine. Actually, Dave was sleeping on the couch while Mary was sleeping in the bedroom. This arrangement had been in place for about six months.

One Thursday night, as Dave was heading out to work the night shift, Mary told him she was going out with the girls. She went to a local club with three friends and they sat and talked. As the night progressed, there ensued dancing, drinking and lots of laughter—just what Mary felt she needed.

The next morning, Dave arrived home from work around 7:15 A.M. Quietly, he walked over to the bedroom, closed the door so he wouldn't wake Mary, then made himself some coffee and crawled onto the couch to get some sleep. Around 12:30 P.M., Mary got out of bed, woke Dave up and told him to sleep in the bed so she could clean the house.

Later that month, Mary said that she was going out with the girls again. It was the fourth time in as many Thursdays. All Dave said was, "I hope you have fun," and off he went to play hockey.

The next day, Dave was on the day shift and decided to come home for lunch, which was a rare occurrence for him. As Dave walked into the apartment, he saw Mary talking on the telephone and heard her laughing. When she saw Dave, Mary said, "Okay, I'll talk to you later," and hung up the telephone.

"Who were you talking to?" Dave asked. "Mom called and asked about a recipe for supper," Mary said, her tone slightly defensive. Dave shrugged his shoulders and thought nothing of it. Mary went into the bedroom and began changing the sheets on the bed.

That night, while Mary was working her late shift, Dave was home and received a couple of telephone calls that were wrong numbers and a couple more that were hang-ups. He gave them little thought, although he did mention them to Mary. Such calls rarely happened after that.

Dave unexpectedly stopped during the day at their apartment twice the following week. One day he'd forgotten some items he needed for work and another time he'd forgotten his lunch. Both days he saw Mary changing the sheets on their bed. This seemed odd to Dave, but, as he wasn't the suspicious type, he didn't think much about it.

One night, Dave was asked to play in a pick-up hockey game with some guys who were acquaintances but not good friends. The men went uptown for a couple of beers after they got off the ice and sat around talking about sports, cars and women.

Barry, a player Dave had never met before, started talking about a friend of his who was dating a married woman who worked at the local hospital. Barry said this woman's husband was always either working or playing sports. They had no children and the husband didn't give her enough attention, he told the group sitting around the table. He mentioned, among other things, how often the woman managed to be free for secret meetings with his friend.

Dave didn't feel comfortable coming right out and asking a stranger about the details of this affair, but he had a weird feeling in his head and stomach. For the first time in their marriage, he had doubts about his wife. For the first time, he felt suspicious. While Dave had been listening to Barry's story, he was also thinking about what was going on in his relationship with Mary.

He realized that Mary had been spending more and more time away from him and that he had been putting more hours and effort into his work than into their relationship. He also remembered that she had been changing their bed sheets more often than she usually did. Their conversation was always boringly the same—the mundane, day-to-day things that happened. They weren't sleeping together. In fact, they just existed as a couple, living in the same apartment as if they were roommates, not husband and wife.

Mary was on edge lately, Dave knew, but he thought this was because of their relationship problems. However, the more he allowed himself to think about it, the more he realized how much her behavior had actually changed in the last few weeks. There was not only the frequent changing of sheets but also the wrong number and hang-up telephone calls to the house and Mary's new routine of trips to bars and clubs with her girlfriends.

No, he thought to himself, *she wouldn't be having an affair.*

Naturally, Dave didn't want to believe Mary was cheating on him. He tried to rationalize his suspicions: *When would she find the time? Where would she do it? Not in our bed! She loves me too much!*

Suddenly, he was thinking things—terrible, hurtful things—about Mary and their relationship that he had never considered before. He began visualizing his wife with another man. He could see her in the arms of a faceless stranger, making love. It turned his stomach. He desperately tried to push such thoughts from his mind as he drove home that night.

The situation between Julie and Ben differs from that of Mary and Dave in several ways. For one thing, Julie felt that she and Ben had a strong relationship and got along extremely well, especially considering Ben's hectic work schedule. Ben was frequently away. He was a good provider, but he was constantly working and rarely home. Julie tried to get Ben to understand that they needed to spend more time together and she told him she didn't want to be just a baby-sitter for his children during their weekend visits.

Still, Ben continued to work many hours and Julie took care of the house on her own. Even when it was time for Ben to spend his visitation with his children, he would sometimes head off to work for the afternoon. Ben insisted to Julie that if he didn't work as hard as he did all the nice things they had accumulated would have to be sold.

Julie very much wanted her relationship with Ben to work. She felt committed for the long haul. Although she wished that some things would change, she didn't question what Ben was doing or why. She knew Ben loved her and there was no denying that he was a good provider. It troubled Julie, though, that whenever she pointed out flaws in their relationship and suggested ways to improve it, Ben just ignored her.

What Julie didn't know was that Ben was having one affair after another. In fact, he had a different woman in several nearby towns. Each of the women knew Ben was living with Julie in a committed relationship but didn't seem to care. Ben was honest with them, treated them nicely and made them laugh. According to the women, he gave them what they wanted and what they needed—affection without any commitment.

Ben would take off at least once a week for an overnight stay, sometimes longer, under the guise of business appointments. Julie hadn't a clue that Ben was having secret, out-of-town rendezvous until she found clear-cut evidence—an incriminating receipt—as she was emptying his trouser pockets one day, getting them ready to be taken to the cleaners.

Devastated, she reflected that she now knew why he was spending so much time away from home. She also had a pretty good idea of how he managed to cheat on her without arousing her suspicions. What troubled her the most, however, was why. Why was he compelled to cheat?

Julie was bitter, hurt and disappointed at what Ben had done and what he had failed to do. She couldn't believe how selfish he had been. All she could think was, *How could he do this to me? How could he do this to our family? He's destroyed so much — and for what? Why didn't I see this coming?*

Married for ten years with two children aged five and seven, Wendy and Liam seemed to have it all. They lived in a beautiful home, drove expensive cars and enjoyed pleasant family vacations together. Wendy was a full-time mom and Liam owned his own successful computer business. Like Ben, Liam worked hard and was often away from home for lengthy periods of time, but he was proud of the fact that his family wanted for nothing and he was an excellent provider.

Despite the fact that Liam and Wendy did not have an exciting sex life — in fact, they had slept together only sporadically over the past few years — Liam still believed his wife was content and he was providing her with everything she needed. Over time, however, certain things occurred which made Liam suspicious. There were strange telephone calls, many hang-ups when Liam picked up the receiver. Wendy's behavior began to seem odd and out of sync with her husband. Finally, he had to admit to himself that he suspected Wendy was having an affair. Reluctantly, he called a private investigator. Liam explained the situation to the investigator and requested a tap on his telephone. That way, he reasoned, he would have irrefutable evidence of cheating, if indeed such a thing were actually going on.

The private investigator explained that the laws in the area did not allow him to tap telephones, but he said he would tell Liam where to buy the equipment himself at low cost, how to set it up and what to do with the evidence. Liam purchased the equipment and installed it the way the private investigator had told him. A few weeks later, Liam called the private investigator and told him about conversations he had recorded between his wife and another man.

On the tape, Wendy and her lover talked about the different ways of making love, how they would schedule their next meeting and how they turned each other on. Liam discovered that Wendy planned to charge up all the credit cards, drain the bank accounts, take the children and move far away from Liam.

Shaken to his very core, it took every bit of strength Liam could muster to keep his composure around Wendy. Until he could formulate how he was going to handle his wife's betrayal, Liam continued to live in the same house as Wendy and went about his daily routine. However, thinking about what she had been doing with someone else tore him apart.

The fact that they had not been sleeping together for some time wasn't the issue, as far as Liam was concerned. Liam loved Wendy, but apparently she didn't have the same feelings for him, he felt; Otherwise she couldn't make love with another man. As much as he tried, Liam could not rationalize his wife's behavior. He couldn't believe Wendy would tear up their family this way.

Liam finally confronted Wendy. She denied the affair and told him he was out of his mind. Liam did not tell Wendy of the evidence he had. Wendy told her husband she sincerely wanted the relationship to work and would attend family counseling with him to save their marriage. Liam felt a little better about this, but was still suspicious. He needed to be sure of Wendy's intentions. And so he hired a private investigator to follow his wife.

Much to the dismay of those who, like Dave, Julie and Liam, are looking for quick answers to the question of why mates cheat, there is no one reason why cheating happens. I have found it to be a combination of three reasons:

1. Emotional Misunderstandings/Lack of Emotions
2. Excitement
3. Ego

Emotional Misunderstandings/Lack of Emotions describe the distortion or deficiency of two necessary ingredients in any relationship: giving and receiving.

An individual's desire to feel needed by others may be a wholesome and endearing trait, yet in the extreme, it may be a backbreaking burden for his or her mate. Similarly, the need to be cared for and nurtured is a universal and healthy human characteristic, unless it is taken to the extreme. In the best case scenario, each partner in a relationship gives himself or herself internal permission to be dependent on each other. This allows each person to lie back, put his or her guard down and be close to another human being. The giver and receiver share a sense of mutual closeness and trust that fosters feelings of safety and intimacy.

When a person desires only to give to a mate or only to receive from him or her, the relationship scale becomes tipped and unbalanced. The joys of everyday mutual giving and receiving are diminished or perhaps may become non-existent when, in fact, the acts of giving and receiving should be shared between the two people.

All too often, the partners begin to distance themselves from each other when their relationship becomes unbalanced in this way. They may stop talking about the personal, joyous and everyday events in their lives and one or both may gradually, over time, become involved with other people who will listen to and sympathize with their problems.

Although the majority of affairs begin in the workplace and often go undetected by cheaters' mates, the signs and signals leading up to infidelities frequently are ignored. There are clues left by potential cheating mates and it is important to be aware of them. These subtle and not-so-subtle signs may be happening right in front of you.

Signs that your mate is thinking about cheating:
- Your mate shares a *common interest* with somebody of the opposite sex. This could be work-related, a course taken with a neighbor or joining a volunteer group and meeting others with similar interests thus involving a great amount of time with this other person and away from you.

- Your mate frequently *compares* you to other people. A faithful mate has no need to compare.

- Your mate makes remarks about how well another person *relates to and understands* him or her. Your partner may think this person is the perfect mate when, in reality, the man or woman is just doing a better job of listening to your mate's needs than you have been.

- Your mate is *enthusiastic* about working late, looks forward to attending particular courses or seminars or is eager to go out for a night on the town without you.

- Your mate starts to show signs of *dishonesty*. For instance, he makes excuses to drive or walk to the corner store for a newspaper so he can use the pay telephone to talk to someone in privacy.

- Your mate continually criticizes another person to you. She may be trying to hide romantic feelings for the other person in this way.

◆ Your mate is very *flirtatious* with an individual while at a party or social event with you. You may notice excessive eye contact between them from across the room or subtle hand gestures or facial expressions.

◆ Your mate tells someone else very *intimate and personal details* about himself or herself, including your relationship together and any past troubles you have experienced as a couple. When your mate exposes such intimacies to another, this emotional betrayal may rapidly lead to a physical betrayal as well.

◆ Your mate *touches* or *hugs* a certain person frequently. An everyday touch of the shoulder or hug at the office or a social gathering may reveal hidden feelings and lead to an affair if your partner is feeling vulnerable.

◆ Your mate begins leaving *discreet messages* or *little gifts* for someone on his desk at work, the windshield of her car or some other special place. Likewise, the other party does the same. Only the prospective cheater will know what these messages and trinkets signify and who they're from, should you happen accidentally to intercept one.

◆ Your mate comes up with *excuses* to be away from you, giving him time to spend with someone else. Such secret meetings only lead to lies and more lies. When this occurs, communication is probably at an all-time low in your relationship with your partner.

Almost every relationship goes through phases where one or the other partner will say, "You really don't care about my feelings" or "I'm not getting what I want." A feeling of attachment, of wanting to belong to someone else, is one reason people fall in love, but if the desire for attachment is excessive, it may hurt the committed relationship over time. When one partner goes beyond close to clingy, it may mean your relationship is based on insecurity and immaturity, not freedom and strength.

Achieving a healthy balance between giving and receiving in a relationship depends to a great deal on open and uncensored communication between the two people involved. Ann Landers has written: "The most sensitive sex organ in men and women is the ear and the most potent aphrodisiac is the spoken word."

Excitement is a need that should not be overlooked when discussing why cheating occurs. When a mate cheats, part of the attraction is that sexually it's a new and different experience. It's also *forbidden*, which may add to the temptation (remember Adam, Eve and the apple!). Like teenagers trying to fool around without getting caught while a parent sits in the next room or couples who enjoy having sex in semi-public places, the risk, the gamble, the tempting of fate adds that certain *frisson* of excitement to sexual experiences for some people.

In its early stages, the excitement of a new and illicit affair can make people do things that are completely out of character for them. They may revert to childish behavior or affect baby talk when speaking to their new lovers, make up silly nicknames and giggle like kids when together. Whenever possible, they will try to be with the new person in their lives…without being caught by their mates.

When your relationship first began with your mate, it was probably as fresh, as invigorating and as exciting as what I have just described. You would have done anything for your mate, anything to make him or her happy and your mate would have done the same for you. Similar feelings are experienced by cheating mates and their lovers, but it's forbidden love and your mate knows it.

Ego, both yours and your mate's, is often overlooked as an integral piece of the cheating puzzle. It's fairly obvious that a new sexual partner is gratifying to a person's ego. Thus, someone who needs an abundance of ego-fulfillment may be more tempted to cheat than someone who doesn't have this need.

However, *your* ego also plays a part in this dynamic. Perhaps your ego prevents you from seeing the signs that your mate is cheating, because you believe so strongly that he or she could not possibly do that to you. Your mate treats you so well and you are so good to him or her in return that you honestly believe this individual would never be unfaithful. Even if you are aware your partner cheated on a past mate, you honestly believe he or she will never cheat on you. That's your ego taking over your thought process.

Your ego is responsible for thoughts like: *My partner loves me too much to ever stray* or *She is so busy with work and the children. How would my mate find the time?* Now ask yourself these questions: *Do I truly know what is going on in my mate's head? Do I know if his needs and desires are truly being met? Am I with my mate every minute, every hour of the day? How much time is needed for a lunch hour assignation or a quickie after work? How long does it actually take?* If you're honest with yourself and put aside your own ego, you will soon realize that cheating can always be managed despite time restraints and even emotional ties to a mate. You are not with your mate twenty-four hours a day. Do you really think that, despite being busy, he or she wouldn't be able to make time for an affair?

A country music song written by Bobby Wood, John Peppard and Garth Brooks, entitled *In Another's Eyes*, gives a suitable description of how your *ego* works. The song is about two separate relationships. In each, one person has no suspicions of their partner's thoughts of leaving.

The words in this song describe how your *ego* tells you that your relationship is perfect and your partner would never cheat or lie when, in fact, he or she is having doubts about the relationship. You're unaware because your relationship brings thoughts of morality and virtue, not doubt and distrust.

Your thoughts run along the lines of: "I've been with him/her too long, I have too much invested in the relationship and I know my mate too well for that to happen." If you think this way, your ego is too big and you'll never be open-minded enough to catch a cheating mate.

My advice is to put aside emotion and ego. Think with your head and use logic when you suspect your mate is cheating. In the following pages, I will show you how.

People who cheat on their mates often are very selfish and think only about themselves and what makes them happy. Cheating frequently is a form of addiction and addicts will say and do whatever it takes to keep their addiction going. In the case of cheaters, they will do whatever is necessary to keep their mates ignorant of their behavior. By their very nature, cheating mates are major manipulators who, like drug addicts or alcoholics, may or may not recognize the damage they are doing to their relationships with their mates but nevertheless must have their next fix.

In my years of investigating such adulterous acts professionally, I've also had friends and acquaintances who were not faithful to their partners. At times, I'd be performing surveillance on a cheating spouse or a fraudulent insurance claim and I'd see someone I knew doing things he or she wasn't supposed to do. Sometimes I'd even see these things when I was off duty. Once, towards the end of a long day, I stopped at a local bar to have a drink and relax before heading home. Sitting there, I saw a man I knew walk into the establishment holding hands with a much younger, very attractive woman. When he recognized me and realized that I had seen them enter, he dropped her hand and approached me. He greeted me and started a casual conversation, but I had the sense that he was trying to get a feel for what I was thinking.

I knew him and his wife quite well and so I asked if they had separated. He said no and explained who the young woman was and intimated that they were having an affair. I wasn't investigating this man; it was pure coincidence that I ran into him at the bar. The point is that things like this have happened before and they will probably happen again.

I saw the man from the bar and his spouse together with their children many times after that. To my knowledge, his wife had no idea that he had an affair. When I saw him alone a few months later, he claimed the extramarital relationship ended shortly after I'd seen him with his lover. He did mention to me, however, that he suspected his wife might be cheating on him. Whether this is true or not, I have no idea. Not surprisingly, when I recently ran into his wife, she told me they were in the process of getting a divorce.

Don't be among those who say they will never need a book about how to catch a cheating mate. Instead, examine the signs your mate exhibits that make you suspicious then apply your gut feeling. Be honest. You know when something is wrong. If you think about it, has your gut ever let you down before?

You must look past your ego, apply common sense and detach yourself from the immediate situation so you can see the whole picture. Try to judge the situation from the outside looking in.

Another way of looking at it is to think of all the people you know who have had a mate cheat on them. What advice would you give to these individuals if you were listening to their stories? Well, just follow your own advice. It's your ego that won't let you see the signs of a cheating mate. *If you don't believe me, then ask somebody who has been cheated on.*

The individual reasons for cheating are numerous, but once analyzed they break down into just a few categories as was previously mentioned: **Emotional Misunderstandings/Lack of Emotions**; the quest for **Excitement**; and the gratification of **Ego**. These are the three main reasons why people think about cheating and, given the opportunity, will betray a mate.

For this book, I surveyed men and women about why they cheated on their mates. Here are some of the most frequent answers broken down by gender:

Women said they cheated for these reasons:

(1)   Lack of communication with him...

(2)   We didn't spend enough quality time together...

(3)   Another man was more understanding when I needed it most...

(4)   Another man was more attractive...

(5)   The sex was terrible and infrequent...

(6)   He cheated on me, so it was payback time...

(7)   He wasn't romantic enough...

(8)   One man couldn't satisfy me enough...

(9)   I just fell out of love with him...

(10) He wasn't sensitive to my needs...

(11) I wanted to see if I was still attractive and sexy to other men...

(12) I was sexually abused when I was younger...

Men said they cheated for these reasons:

(1)   All she did was nag, nag, nag...

(2)   She never wanted to have sex...

(3)   We were fighting too much and one night this girl was too good-looking to pass up...

(4)   She gained too much weight...

(5)   It's in our genes to run wild...

(6)   Our sex life was really boring...

(7)   I needed an ego boost and somebody to make me feel like a man...

(8)   She turned me off after the baby was born...

(9)   She was always putting me down. No matter what I did for her, it was never enough...

(10) I just didn't want to be with her anymore...

(11) We both were going in different directions in our lives...

(12) I was sexually abused as a child...

After all you've read thus far, what reasons do you think your partner might have for cheating on you? List them on the following page.

Reasons Why My Mate Might Cheat

1._____

_____

_____

_____

2._____

_____

_____

_____

3._____

_____

_____

_____

4._____

_____

_____

_____

Some thoughts from Dr. Weiner:

People who cheat, while differing in personality, all have something in common. They are addicts. Despite the protestations, denials and pointing of fingers elsewhere, as with all addicts, at the first sign of discomfort, they run for their fix. In these cases, it is to the affair. And an illicit relationship can be found anywhere, at any time, as well as with anyone. The cheater can be away on a business trip, taking a night course, participating in his or her own wedding or finding an opportunity in the lavatory of an airplane. All these situations are not uncommon. For these addicts, the marital/relationship "itches" are lifelong: be it after one year (73 percent of men who commit adultery do so after two or more years of marriage, while another 23 percent of men who have affairs begin them before their second wedding anniversary) or be it after seven or twenty or more. When it "itches," such individuals scratch. Of course, all too often, this only leads to more "itching!"

With the advent of Viagra and the current push that it be offered to women as well as men, the opportunities for sexual experiences are endless. The male of seventy or eighty years of age, no longer able to rely on the taken-for-granted erection, can now feel as though he is still in the prime of his life. Indeed, Ponce de Leon's Fountain of Youth is right there in his own medicine cabinet, available whenever he needs it. And the woman? If she was formerly considered non-sexual or disinterested in sex, she can now indulge and be part of the super-cool, sexually charged culture she perhaps once played little or no role in. With their worlds opened up and senses on fire, men and women may play farther afield, with the result that the marital bed comes in a poor second. "Pleasure take all" is the motto and moral values are overthrown and tossed away like a worn garment. Consequences for a spouse, a long-term lover or the children are seemingly dismissed.

Nothing can or does interrupt the cheater's pleasure. However, there are always consequences. And for the most part, the consequences are devastating to all in the player's court.

The question then arises: Can a leopard change his/her spots? Not unless the leopard becomes aware of the spots and wants to do something about them. But if a mate is unwilling to make the change, what can you, the betrayed partner, do? You can be alerted to the manifest signs of deception and then take action. It is you who will make the changes—in whatever direction you see fit. The next chapter clearly describes when cheating is most likely to occur and the chapter after that lists the 180 telltale signs of deception. You owe it to yourself to know them.

❖

chapter three

❖

When Cheating is Most Likely to Occur

Cheating by a partner can happen at any time and in many circumstances during the term of a relationship.

In Mary and Dave's marriage, Mary found plenty of time in which to cheat because of her and her husband's conflicting work schedules. They were rarely home together at the same time. Even when they both had free time, they seemed to go in opposite directions: Dave to a hockey game, Mary out with her friends.

Mary felt her marriage wasn't a marriage at all. "We were roommates—friends or acquaintances. We weren't lovers!" She understood about good times and bad times. She had heard and read about people who have affairs and the damage an affair does to a relationship. Mary says she wasn't looking to become a statistic.

"Dave and I were drifting apart for years," Mary said. "We both were set in our ways." Mary felt she needed more attention. When she made subtle suggestions to Dave, he would just question her motives. Either they'd just have sex or Dave would tell her he was late for work and out the door he'd go.

Mary said she started to do other things to fill her time, such as bingo, crafts and work. She spent most of her time with family until one night she went to the club with a bunch of girlfriends. She had too much to drink and this one guy, Kevin, was paying attention to her.

Mary said that she talked to Kevin about relationships and how hers was failing. Kevin wasn't the attractive, macho type that Dave was, but he was understanding and appeared to take a deep interest in Mary as a person—attention she wasn't getting from Dave.

Mary had been faithful to every person she had ever dated. Cheating was never an option in her mind, but Kevin was telling Mary everything she needed to hear. Kevin began calling Mary at work and, on occasion, at home. Kevin had hung up on Dave a couple of times and asked for somebody who didn't live there so as not to arouse any suspicions from Dave.

Kevin and Mary had lengthy phone conversations when she was at work, usually in the early morning hours when her patients were sleeping. Mary said it was exciting and playful. She didn't think anything of it at the time.

However, the talks between them became more and more personal. It was like two school children in a new relationship. Mary said they flirted and eventually talked about sex. Mary began telling secrets to Kevin that even Dave didn't know.

Mary didn't realize it at first, but she came to understand she was having an emotional affair that would eventually turn into a physical affair. She saw too late that she should have turned to Dave and been honest with him. Marital counseling was something they both should have tried.

Mary and Kevin would meet for coffee at a restaurant out of town and talk during the day when Dave was at work. It was getting to the point that Mary was excited when she was on her way to meet Kevin. She distanced herself even more from Dave and looked forward to the secret meetings.

Mary remembers clearly the first time it happened. She and Kevin had both agreed to meet at a motel in the early afternoon. Kevin would rent the room and Mary would show up later. Mary says, "It was exciting, yet awkward and scary."

She thought to herself, "I've always been faithful and I love Dave very much, so why am I attracted to Kevin?" What was it that Kevin had that Dave didn't? Why did she want to be with Kevin so badly that she would break her marriage vows?

That Mary had not slept with Dave in months was a factor, but it wasn't the main reason. It was because Kevin paid attention to her. He gave her what Dave did not. Kevin was understanding, thoughtful and exciting. Kevin was all the things Dave used to be and more. Or so Mary thought.

Mary said that after the first time she had sex with Kevin, she knew it was wrong. She cried when she got home because of the guilt she felt inside. She had done something that would distance her husband Dave from her forever and she knew it. She had crossed that line, but reasoned with herself that what Dave didn't know would never hurt him.

That first occasion was supposed to be a one-time fling. It wasn't meant to be an ongoing affair. She just needed something new for that moment, Mary thought. Kevin, on the other hand, kept calling. One meeting led to several meetings until Mary admitted to herself that she had feelings for both men.

Seventy-seven percent of women who cheat fall in love, while only 43 percent of men do.

Passionate promiscuity and one-night stands are very stimulating when someone envisions them. The truth is that long-term emotional cheating, which is what Mary was doing, ruins more relationships than one-night stands.

Cheating can be woven into the fabric of relationships everywhere. It happens during marriages and both short and long-term relationships. Julie and Ben had a good relationship, yet cheating seemed to be encoded on one of Ben's genes. It was simply a part of who he was.

Julie only became suspicious when she was cleaning out Ben's pants' pockets before taking them to the cleaners. In one of his pockets, she found a receipt for an out-of-town restaurant that said "2 Guests" at the top. The bill was over a hundred dollars. In another pocket was a scrap piece of paper with a faded telephone number on it.

Julie called the number and a woman answered the telephone. When Julie quickly made up a name and asked to speak to the fictitious person, she was told she had the wrong number.

Julie decided that before she confronted Ben, she would wait and see if anything else suspicious turned up. She'd learned how to catch a cheat from her first marriage. Her former husband had an affair while they were married and now she had a gut feeling that it was happening again. She knew that if you want to catch a cheating mate, you can't let him know you're on to him. If you do, the cheater will go to greater lengths to hide the affair.

Ben, it turned out, was sending all his mail to a post office box. His secretary would pick up the mail and place it on Ben's desk. Ben would then get his secretary to pay the bills. He told her what the amount of each would be so she never needed to see the detailed billing.

Julie told his secretary that she was going to surprise Ben with a package that would soon arrive at his post office box, because she didn't want it to arrive at home. She told the secretary she would pick up the mail for the next two weeks and drop it off to her at a meeting place outside the office. Julie and the secretary agreed that neither Ben nor any co-workers would know about it so the birthday surprise wouldn't be ruined.

The surprise was on Ben. Julie read Ben's detailed cellular billing, plus letters from three of his mistresses. The letters were very descriptive. They contained information about when Ben had been out of town, where he had stayed and what he had done with them. It also had the women's names, addresses and telephone numbers. One letter was from Julie's best friend, Betty, who was also married and lived on the outskirts of town.

Julie was heartbroken. She cried because Ben had promised he would never do the things her first husband had done. Julie couldn't believe Ben would cheat on her. When Julie stopped crying, she began to plan how to leave.

Julie waited for Ben to take another of his out-of-town trips. As soon as he left the house, the moving trucks arrived. She moved everything they owned into a new apartment she had rented. She disconnected their telephone and got an unlisted telephone number. She then transferred her daughter out of the local school and registered her in one near where she had moved.

When I interviewed Ben, he told me he had had frequent affairs. He said if you traveled often, especially to the same places on a regular basis, it made it easier to establish relationships. He said he had used his mistresses as emotional crutches. Ben insisted he had always been honest with the women with whom he was having affairs. "I always told them I was involved in a long-term relationship," he said. Unfortunately, he wasn't as honest with Julie.

When Julie found out about his cheating and moved out, it didn't seem to bother him very much. At the time, it almost appeared as if he were looking for a way out of their relationship. But as time passed, life just wasn't the same for Ben and he realized too late the valuable relationship he had with Julie.

The last time I spoke with Ben, he told me, "I just never thought about how much emotional pain I was inflicting on Julie, whom I love. And it's not only Julie I hurt, but her daughter as well. Cheating is a selfish act that satisfied my ego. Being tempted to cheat is a test of a person's integrity. I'm afraid I failed the test."

Both Mary and Ben were sorry and repentant after their infidelities were discovered, unlike Wendy, Liam's wife. Although she agreed to go to counseling after Liam confronted her about his suspicion she was cheating, her heart wasn't in it.

Liam wanted her followed on the nights she was attending counseling sessions by herself and he hired a private investigator. The investigator followed her from her home to the counseling office and waited outside. About an hour-and-a-half later, Wendy emerged from her session. She had a brief conversation with a few people outside and left the area in her vehicle. The investigator again picked up the trail.

Wendy drove to a local coffee shop and parked at the back of the building. Another car, driven by a man, drove up, parked and the driver got into Wendy's car.

Then Wendy and the man drove to well-known lovers' lane located in a landscaped area that overlooked the city. The two sat in the car and spoke for at least thirty minutes. The investigator's report (condensed version) tells the rest of the story.

The passenger seat of the vehicle was reclined and Wendy moved in between the man's legs. The inside of the car was illuminated when other vehicles drove by and parked in the area. The investigator observed that Wendy was naked and she was performing oral sex on her lover.

The investigator moved to get a better view for his client and observed that Wendy had put on her coat to cover the top half of her body. The investigator observed Wendy straddle the man and noted the time. Seconds later, after observing Wendy go up and down eight times, she climbed off her lover and sat in the driver's seat. The investigator made a note of the time.

The investigator waited for two minutes and then left the area. The investigator drove to the rear of the restaurant and, approximately two minutes later, Wendy dropped off her lover. The investigator followed as Wendy stopped at a convenience store, picked up some milk and then arrived home around 1:00 A.M.

The next day, the investigator had a meeting with Liam. The information was passed on and a copy of the report was also supplied to Liam's lawyer. Liam shook with rage and the investigator warned Liam not to do anything rash.

Liam confronted Wendy with the evidence of her infidelity and demanded a divorce, yet she was not contrite. In fact, Wendy did not take any responsibility for the break-up of her marriage. Rather, she blamed the private investigator for breaking up her marriage!

When and under what conditions is cheating most likely to occur? Common times for cheating are:

- The beginning of a relationship

- After the first year of the relationship

- During business trips away from home

- The bachelor or bachelorette party

- The wedding

- The first year of marriage

- During pregnancy

- After the birth of a child

- The four-year itch

- The seven-year itch

- During a mid-life crisis

The Beginning of a Relationship

This often occurs when one person is on the rebound from a past relationship and still has feelings for his or her former lover, especially when one relationship quickly follows the other.

The new relationship may be exciting but strong feelings for the past lover still linger. The person and his or her lover from the old relationship may maintain contact and may even have sex several more times. Comparisons may be made between the past and present partners.

After The First Year of the Relationship

At this time in a relationship, the couple has usually worked out all the kinks and quirks about each other. Sex possibly has lost the spark of the new and exciting.

In many situations, due to the hectic schedule of both parties, making love has to be done before ten o'clock in order to get a good night's sleep. Heaven forbid you disturb each other after midnight. Couples know each other quite well by this time and have already fought about the position of the toilet seat. They don't necessarily live together, but one or the other will stay overnight from time to time. In other words, even if they are not married, the relationship has settled into a domestic routine.

During Business Trips Away From Home

This can be either a one-night stand or a longer relationship when a person routinely visits another geographical area for work or other reasons.

When a person stays in a motel or hotel after a long day on the road or trapped in numerous, dull business meetings, a visit to the hotel bar might occur. This can lead to conversations between consenting adults, which may lead to a drink, which may lead to dinner and, if there are problems or discontentment in the committed relationship, sex.

The Bachelor or Bachelorette Party

This is a time when drunkenness prevails and friends are encouraging the honored bachelor or bachelorette to do things he or she wouldn't normally do. Alcohol clouds judgment, but it is no excuse to cheat on a fiancée.

A man might be made to feel that this is the last time he will be free to have sex with others. The man's friends may tease him openly about having sex with only one woman for the rest of his life, telling him he might as well take his last chance.

A woman may be urged to do something, because it's the last time she'll have the opportunity to be with another man legitimately. A male stripper may take her aside in a room alone for a private dance that may be pre-arranged. She will think, *What the heck, nobody will see me and they'll assume he's just dancing seductively for me.* If the wedding is a few weeks away, a second, secret meeting might be set up with the dancer.

The Wedding

Cheating may take place either the night before the wedding or even the day of, especially during the reception. The participants in the liaison can include the bride, the groom or a wedding guest. Perhaps it's the emotionally charged events of the day, the finality—in terms of sexual relationships—of marriage, the revelry after the ceremony or excessive alcohol consumption, but whatever the reason, cheating on a mate is surprisingly commonplace at weddings.

If it's the bride or the groom cheating, then sex will definitely be quick, as they don't want to arouse suspicions by being missed. If a wedding guest is going to cheat on his or her mate, then it usually will take place at the reception or somewhere in the vicinity. It could be in a car, the lawn, the parking lot (car), a back room, the bathroom, motel or hotel room or, if a trip back to the family home is in store, it may take place there.

The First Year of Marriage

This is the time in a relationship when all the excitement that has been surrounding the couple begins to quiet down. Problems in the first year of marriage often center on the couples' immaturity, lack of readiness and sexual difficulties.

A man may have an affair because he feels that he has to prove he can still seduce or be attractive to another woman. On the other hand, a young wife may not find her husband as attentive as when they were dating and first married. She still needs and wants attention, though, and another man might fulfill her needs, if only momentarily.

Flirtations or brief affairs are rarely discovered, but they can lead to additional affairs or long-term adulterous relationships later on.

During Pregnancy

In this cheating scenario, it's usually the man who strays. If a woman strays, it will be at the early stage of her pregnancy, most likely because her mate is not supporting her emotionally at a time when she needs it the most. Also, she may not be aware of the pregnancy and not realize why her emotions seem topsy-turvy. Once the pregnancy is confirmed, a woman usually will not risk any negative health issues when it comes to her child.

Some men find it a turn-off to make love to a pregnant woman. Others become selfishly fed up with the complaints, the requests for back and foot rubs and the demands to help with the chores around the house. In the later stages of the pregnancy, a man may look elsewhere for a woman to keep him sexually content after he's been cut off from sex with his partner.

A man might indulge in a one-night stand, which may turn into a longer affair. On some occasions, the man may turn to a prostitute.

After The Birth of A Child

It's common for infidelity to occur after the birth of a couple's first child. The birth of a second child doesn't seem to jolt a relationship to the same degree.

Men and women differ in their reasons for beginning an affair at this time. A man may feel cheated, because his mate is either giving all her attention to the newborn or doesn't seem interested in sex anymore. She may not be the same woman after the child's birth that he envisioned she was. Also, for some men, it is a sexual turn-off to view the birth of the baby. The desire he once had for his mate may be tainted by his new view of her as a mother.

A woman will notice very quickly if her partner shows no interest in her and the newborn child. She may have a strong need for attention and, when she feels it is lacking in the relationship, she may seek it through time spent with another man, possibly one she meets at work or during a night out with her girlfriends.

The Four-Year Itch

Problems with fidelity often occur when a couple has been married for four years with one child. If a second child is not imminent, this seems to be the time when any marriage problems or doubts about the relationship will surface.

One spouse might make a decision to end the relationship while the other has no idea his or her partner is harboring doubts. The unhappy mate may see his or her spouse and their lifestyle together as very boring and mundane. Communication possibly will have broken down to an all-time low, perhaps completely. At a time like this, another person showing interest in the discontented partner may be all it takes to plunge him or her into an affair.

The Seven-Year Itch

Many people think relationships will either come to a stop at or continue forever after the seven-year-itch mark, depending on the state of the relationship. After seven years, a partner may be unfaithful due to boredom. Some people seem to think the relationship, at this point, has gone through all the development it can and there is nothing new on the horizon.

There has been a marriage, probably children, a new car or mini-van and a new house. Maybe the last step up that career ladder has been earned. People ask themselves: "Have I done everything I wanted to do? Is there something else left in life? Am I missing something or is this all there is?"

The most common time for cheating is when this type of thinking prevails; it makes an individual very susceptible to temptation. An affair during this phase of a relationship often causes strong feelings between the cheater and his or her lover. It is likely this person will either have a long-lasting affair or end the original relationship.

Even if there has been clear sailing in a relationship so far, this is the time when problems may begin.

During a Mid-Life Crisis

Affairs often occur at this emotionally precarious time precisely because of all the years invested in the relationship. Everything that can happen has happened. The children have grown up, the house has been paid for, the job is mundane, the car is changed every five years and the sex is routine. A person may feel nothing is left except spending stale time alone with their mate for the rest of their lives. *Is this all there is?* becomes a common refrain.

Middle-aged men generally experience increases in tenderness and intimacy along with a decrease in sexual assertiveness. They become more relationship-oriented. Middle-aged women, on the other hand, often feel more confident and become more sexually assertive.

A redefinition and restating of each partner's sexual needs may be necessary at this juncture. People who stray at this time often will either have a quick fling or involve themselves in round after round of casual sex in an attempt to feel and look younger and relieve the boredom they feel permeates their lives. Some men want to prove their sexual prowess to themselves and society, while some women want to prove their sexual desirability to themselves and their mate.

Both sexes often behave differently, bringing noticeable changes to their lifestyles. You know your mate better than anyone does, so when he or she begins to think about or indulges in an affair in mid-life, you should notice the differences. He or she may lose weight, start exercising, buy new clothes, get a trendy new hairstyle, buy a new cologne or perfume, listen to newer music and, in general, start acting like a younger, hipper version of him/herself.

Common circumstances that contribute to cheating are:

+ Living in different cities

+ Couples that often socialize

+ Low maturity level/young age at marriage

+ Moving or employment change (promotion/demotion)

+ Disability/chronic illness/death

+ Financial problems

+ Retirement or losing a job

+ Second marriages

* Close work relationships

* Having a best friend of the opposite sex

* Alcoholism, drug use or gambling

* Playing team sports

* When a mate takes a night course or returns to school

* Domestic violence

* Close relationships with in-laws

Living in Different Cities

This type of long-distance relationship is very difficult to sustain for any length of time. Absence is said to make the heart grow fonder, but over a long period of time it's not unusual for one partner (or both) to find someone nearby to meet his or her needs. The lonely or discontented partner may be innocently seeking out friendly companionship at the start, but eventually, because his or her emotional and physical needs aren't being satisfied fully, the individual may succumb to temptation and cheat.

Couples that Often Socialize Together

An attraction between two people who often socialize together with their respective mates is often as undetectable as a work-related affair, providing the participants are discreet. It may be a short-term or long-term relationship. It may be a one-night-stand. Obviously, if the affair is discovered by one or both of the other mates, the friendship between the couples is compromised. However, even if it's not revealed, the couples' friendship may end or become more distant because of the guilty feelings of the two lovers or because their affair has ended.

Low Maturity Level / Young Age At Marriage

When an individual is very young, he or she might not be mature enough to understand the commitment that marriage or an exclusive relationship demands. A person who marries or enters into a long-term relationship at a young age, especially one who has been intimate with only that one person, is more likely to have an affair than a person who makes that commitment at a more mature age.

My research and experience shows that many young people really need to sow their wild oats before committing to other people. Generally, the younger people are when they become involved in serious relationships, the less wisdom they have and the more likely they will be to experiment with other partners later in life.

Moving or Employment Change (Promotion / Demotion)

Radical changes in employment often put new pressures on a relationship. If a mate has been promoted or demoted, changes are coming. Promotion often brings celebrations and a raise in pay; However, the downside is longer hours, more stress and additional time spent away from a partner, which may fuel unrest in the relationship.

Demotion or loss of employment frequently brings depression, anxiety and bitterness. This may be especially significant when the other partner continues to work. The added stress sometimes causes the unemployed mate to seek attention elsewhere, which may be due to resentment of the working partner, general unhappiness or depression and an excessive amount of free time.

A change at work might require moving to another state or country, which also can cause turmoil, especially if the promoted mate is too busy or distracted to contribute to the relationship. If relocation is necessary, the couple might have to live apart until the other partner can find work in the same area, leaving both mates susceptible to cheating.

Disability / Chronic Illness / Death

A person who has to deal with a serious or terminal illness, disability or death in the family, has quite a burden on his or her shoulders. It can be a burden that often becomes too great to bear alone. If an individual feels his or her mate isn't comforting or supportive enough, he or she may seek the attentions of someone else.

While a comforting, sympathetic conversation may be all the person needs to feel better, any ego boost or emotional connection at this time has the possibility of leading to an affair because of the individual's vulnerability.

Financial Problems

When a couple has money problems and creditors are calling constantly for cash that neither partner has, it's frustrating and stressful. Both individuals may be working very hard to get debt-free, but they are just treading water and never getting ahead of their financial obligations. When one partner is constantly working, an affair might begin with a co-worker; the other partner, feeling neglected, may also be tempted to cheat. Hidden vices, such as drinking heavily or a gambling addiction, only compound the problem.

The stress of financial problems can lead to cheating; However, the second leading cause of marital break-ups *after* infidelity is money problems.

Retirement or Losing a Job

When a job or career has ended, a man or woman may be feeling insecure and vulnerable. With plenty of free time and few commitments, as well as new friction with his or her mate, the unemployed partner may begin an affair.

Second Marriages

If someone has cheated in his or her first marriage, there's a good chance he or she also will have an affair in the second marriage. It is always hoped that people who get married a second time learn from their mistakes, but, unfortunately, statistics show that 60 percent of second marriages end in divorce.

The common adage, "a leopard doesn't change its spots," certainly applies to individuals who are chronic cheaters. For such individuals, cheating is an addiction, like alcoholism.

Close Work Relationships

An office romance can blossom when an individual is not communicating with a mate or getting the attention he or she needs at home. Such people are vulnerable to any ego building or seductive behavior by a co-worker.

The workplace frequently is where many people spend most of their time. Often, they spend more time there than with their families or mates. A workplace affair is the most common type of affair (49 percent of extramarital relationships were work-related, according to a 2001 survey by Gestner Wren) and one of the most difficult to detect. There are legitimate reasons for the two lovers to be together and the secrecy, ambiguity, competition and politics of workplace life can make it seem especially exciting and sexy.

If your mate is constantly talking about a co-worker of the opposite sex and they work late together often, be very wary. Most people who have work-related affairs do not go into it with their eyes wide open. They often don't understand the ramifications of having their affairs exposed. They might lose their jobs and, even if they don't, they will have to deal with awkward feelings or worse when the romances end, especially if they must continue to work together with their former lovers.

Having a Best Friend of the Opposite Sex

Men and women can be friends on a platonic level, but all too often one person will develop an attraction to the other and want to have a more intimate relationship or possibly sex.

A close friend of the opposite sex is privy to a man's or woman's emotions and feelings and is aware of how that person is treated by his or her mate. The friend will always be there for that individual, always be a shoulder to cry on or someone to commiserate with any time the relationship is in trouble. It puts a lot of temptation in front of them and often people succumb.

Alcoholism, Drug Use and Gambling
The problems that addictions create in committed relationships are more prevalent and more serious than many people realize. Such addictions often go undetected until they've escalated to the point of sheer desperation in the individual and the destruction of his or her relationship.

Like a cheating mate, the addict tries to hide his or her secret until the truth inevitably comes out. Surprisingly, however, it's not usually the addicted person who cheats. More often, the mate who is forced to deal with the behavior of the addict becomes frustrated and unhappy. This may lead to the mate's looking elsewhere for romance and companionship. When this happens, cheating is almost inevitable.

Playing Team Sports
When a person is on a sports team such as hockey, baseball or soccer, be assured that post-game social gatherings will take place from time to time. While socializing with others doesn't necessarily mean a mate will cheat, frequent partying after games and sharing a common bond and interest—in this case, the sports team—may lead to meeting an old flame or finding a new one among the team members or its supporters. An argument at home, dissatisfaction with the committed relationship or a few too many drinks may be all it takes to push the person over the edge and into an affair.

Night Courses or Returning to School

When one partner takes continuing education classes or returns to school for a degree, he or she may find opportunities for cheating in study group meetings or while receiving extra help from a professor, instructor or another student. The cheater usually will discourage a mate from joining him or her in school social activities.

When one partner fraternizes with other students or instructors of a class on a regular basis, small comparisons may be made as he or she may find one of them fascinating. The at-home partner will never know until after it happens.

Domestic Violence

Although there are cases of men being physically abused, in the majority of domestic violence cases, it's the woman who is harmed. Beatings and threats of violence are used to keep her from leaving the relationship.

Generally, an abused woman will have an affair with a person she believes she can trust and who will pay attention to her needs and help her get out of the abusive relationship. When she finds that individual, she may leave her violent mate shortly thereafter.

The abusive male may cheat when the opportunity arises. When he does cheat, the partner rarely knows about it, because the abuser comes and goes as he pleases. If he feels any guilt, he'll often blame his partner and start an argument.

Close Relationships with In-laws

This type of affair is rare and usually revenge-motivated. It happens when one sibling is jealous of another, perhaps because of his or her lifestyle or attractive mate, and proceeds to try to seduce the sibling's partner.

An affair between in-laws also may occur when an individual's marriage is in trouble and his or her sibling tries to mediate or mend the relationship by intervening. An attraction that has been suppressed may suddenly flare up between the helpful sibling and the in-law.

This is a somewhat extensive list but is by no means totally comprehensive. I'm always learning about new, creative and often surprising ways and methods of cheating. This list, however, comprises the most likely times and life circumstances that lead to infidelity and betrayal.

Now that you have read about the common times and circumstances that contribute to adulterous relationships, which ones do you see as relevant to your relationship with your partner? What opportunities or circumstances can you think of that may increase the likelihood of your mate cheating on you? Think about it and don't rule out anything without careful consideration. Write down all possibilities on the list that follows.

Opportunities My Mate Might Be Using for Cheating

1._____

_____

_____

2._____

_____

_____

3._____

_____

_____

4._____

_____

_____

5._____

_____

_____

6._____

_____

_____

7._____

_____

_____

❖

chapter four

❖

The 180 Telltale
Signs of Deception

The techniques and tactics used to deceive mates vary. The signs may be hidden or right in front of you. Only you can pick up many of them, because *you know your mate better than anybody.* If you are observant, what, when, where, why and how your mate does things can tell you when something isn't right.

If David had been a bit more suspicious, the odd telephone calls—the hang-ups, the wrong numbers—might have alerted him to Mary's infidelity. The fact that his wife seemed to be changing the sheets on their bed much more often than usual also should have struck a chord in David's mind. However, David was a trusting soul, he loved Mary and, perhaps, was in denial. It took a figurative slap in the face for David to own up to what was happening in his marriage.

One night, Dave had a hockey game, but when he got to the arena he found out the game had been cancelled. Mary already had left for work and she was supposed to be working all night. Dave left the arena and headed home, but changed his mind and headed for their friend Steve's house. He wanted to talk to him about a surprise birthday party he was planning for Mary.

Dave hoped giving Mary a big birthday party would be the beginning of a better relationship between the two of them. He also planned to cut back on his hours of work and hockey playing in order to spend more time with her. The only reason he played so much hockey, he reasoned, was because of Mary's work schedule. He was bored and did it to fill the time he spent alone.

When he arrived at Steve's place, Dave noticed Mary's car parked in front. He immediately thought, *Steve's house is on her way to work. Maybe her car broke down and she needed a lift.*

Suddenly, Dave remembered what Barry had said about a friend of his dating a married woman—a woman who worked at the hospital. Although the lights were on in Steve's house, Dave couldn't see through the filmy curtains. Dave knocked on the back door. No answer. He tried to open the door. Locked. He finally walked around to the front and knocked on the front window. Still no answer.

In his gut, Dave felt a sinking feeling and knew that something was wrong. There is nothing worse than suspecting something but being unable to prove it. All he could think about was Steve and Mary having an affair. His mind was racing and his stomach was in knots. He reached for his cell phone and called the hospital to find out if Mary was working. The head of her department told him she wasn't there—she'd taken a sick day.

That was all the proof Dave needed. He could no longer pretend there was nothing suspicious in Mary's recent behavior. But how was he going to catch her and her lover? He decided to sit in his car down the road and wait for Mary to emerge from Steve's house. Then he would pounce!

All the while Dave waited, rage built up inside him. All his thoughts were about Steve and Mary together. How long had they been doing this behind his back? How could they? How could she?

About thirty minutes had passed when Steve drove up and pulled into his driveway. Puzzled, Dave drove up right behind him, got out of his car and asked Steve why Mary's car was parked in front of his house. Steve said he didn't know. "Let's go inside and talk about it," Dave said.

Inside, after a brief conversation, the truth was revealed. Mary was having an affair, but it wasn't with Steve. He just knew about it. He even disagreed with her behavior, but he was a friend of Mary's and did not want to get involved. Steve felt cheating was Mary's choice to make, although he said he had warned her that she would also have to live with the consequences of that choice.

According to Dave, it's one thing to suspect your mate is having an affair, but to actually discover it's true feels worse than the death of a friend or loved one. If the loved one dies, you never forget the happy times you spent together. Good memories linger and, eventually, you move on.

But when you're cheated on, the pain seems like it will never go away. The hurt and bitterness you feel last a very long time. Even if you end the relationship, there will always be distasteful, painful memories, especially if you've caught your mate and his/her lover in the act. Such an image will prey on your mind for a very long time. As if these harsh memories aren't bad enough, the person who betrayed you is still alive and well and may live or work near you. You may bump into him at the grocery store or see her in a restaurant with her new love, which makes it that much more difficult to ease the pain and move on with your life.

Ben conducted his illicit affairs very carefully. Other than his frequent trips away from home—and these were business trips, he continually reminded Julie, which allowed them to enjoy a high standard of living—there was no indication that he was cheating.

Julie, who was probably more attuned than others to a mate's suspicious behavior because of her ex-husband's cheating, had no idea that Ben was unfaithful until the day she stuck her hand into his pants pocket and pulled out the tiny pieces of paper that would shatter her trust in Ben forever. Julie was neither obtuse nor in denial. And once she found these two signs of deception, she sprang into action and discovered the truth.

The signs of deception were not as obvious in the case of Liam and Wendy, but Liam acted on his gut feelings. He simply felt there was something odd about Wendy's behavior and this, coupled with a number of hang-up telephone calls he received at their home, made Liam suspicious. He wasted no time and hired a private investigator, who instructed him on how to tap their telephone. What Liam learned from the phone tapes confirmed his worst suspicions. Even after Wendy agreed to attend counseling sessions, Liam still felt uneasy about her conduct and instructed the private investigator to follow her. Unfortunately, his worst suspicions were confirmed.

Liam was not able to be explicit about the signs of deception that he, perhaps instinctively, recognized. He couldn't quite articulate them, but he trusted his gut and therefore learned the devastating truth.

However, even very obvious signs of cheating are sometimes overlooked or denied by people involved in relationships. If your mate exhibits a few of the telltale signs I am about to discuss, it doesn't necessarily mean he or she is cheating. If a number of them apply to your partner, however, you should re-evaluate your relationship and know for what to watch. Once you begin looking more closely and paying stricter attention, you may discover significantly more signs than you initially noticed.

Signs of Cheating

If your partner *consistently* displays six or more of these signs, it would be in your best interest to look further into his or her activities. The signs of cheating can be broken down into three categories:

- **Hidden Signs**

- **Emotional Signs**

- **Physical Evidence**

THE HIDDEN SIGNS

1. Your mate often comes home late, is always having vehicle troubles or has frequent unexplained absences.

2. Your mate wants your home telephone number unlisted or placed in your name only.

3. Your mate buys a cell phone or pager without having a justifiable reason or says his/her employment demands it and neglects to give you the cell phone or pager number.

4. Your mate secretly buys a cell phone or pager and hides it from you.

5. Your mate gets a pager and always keeps it on vibrate mode.

6. Your mate turns off his cell phone or doesn't answer it whenever you are around. (One cheater used to turn his car phone off when he was with his wife. His wife caught him when the caller I.D. on his car phone was not erased and she saw a strange telephone number. She called the number and found herself talking to his girlfriend.)

7. Your mate turns off her pager or doesn't answer pages when you're together.

8. Your mate has a cell phone or pager and it rings or beeps in the wee hours of the morning. If this happens to you, ask your partner who called and pay close attention to the answer.

9. Your mate decides no longer to have a landline telephone. He decides to get just a cell phone or pager (or both) which allows calls to be answered whenever or wherever he wants. In this way, his location is not revealed. ("Of course I'm at the office. Why do you ask?")

10. You receive hang-up telephone calls on a regular basis.

11. You receive an unusually large number of telephone calls that are wrong numbers.

12. Your mate is always the first one to answer the telephone and hangs up quickly if you are nearby.

13. Your mate erases the telephone answering machine messages before you have a chance to hear them.

14. Your mate calls home to listen to the answering machine messages more than twice in an evening. Unless an important call is expected, excessive checking is unnecessary.

15. Your mate won't listen to his or her telephone messages while you're in the vicinity and, if you live separately, your mate's telephone is suddenly off limits for you to answer.

16. Your mate is constantly listening to your answering machine messages. This is a sign of jealousy, but can also reassure an insecure cheater that his or her mate also isn't being unfaithful.

17. Your mate first checks caller I.D. when the telephone rings and sometimes doesn't pick up the telephone.

18. Your mate repeatedly checks the caller I.D. at your place. This also can be a sign of jealousy or it can be reassurance for a cheating mate that you're not cheating.

19. Your mate checks the caller I.D. and erases the names/telephone numbers before you've had a chance to see it.

20. You notice a service charge on your telephone bill for finding the last number that called your residence, because your partner checked to see who a previous caller was. A cheating mate will often do this, because his or her own infidelity has kindled feelings of insecurity.

21. Your mate calls her answering machine from your home, listens to the first part of the message on the speakerphone and then picks up before the messages start.

22. When talking on the telephone, your mate whispers, gives short yes-or-no type answers or abruptly changes the topic of conversation when you enter the room.

23. Your mate stays away from you (walks and stretches the telephone cord a distance) when talking on the telephone.

24. Your mate tells you she has to make a call to a relative, friend or employer and does so at a very peculiar time, often leaving the room.

25. Your mate is frequently spotted using a public telephone. (Take note of the phone location in case surveillance is needed later.)

26. Your mate constantly calls to make sure you're at home. This is a sign of jealousy, but also reassures the cheater that you're not out looking for him when he is out cheating.

27. Your mate has a special night out when she is not to be bothered at all. This could be a set evening for secret meetings with lovers.

28. You occasionally travel out of town overnight for business and your mate continually asks you when and how long you'll be gone and exactly when you will be returning.

29. You make a surprise visit to your mate's workplace and she is not there and no one seems to know where your partner has gone or seems to be covering something up.

30. Your mate either avoids going to work or quits. This could be because an office romance has ended and it's become awkward to see his former lover every day.

31. Your mate is often late getting home from work and has no worthy or reasonable excuses.

32. Your mate shares a common interest with an employee or co-worker of the opposite sex and often spends time with him or her, using their shared interest as the reason.

33. Your mate begins to take a new interest in his or her physical appearance by working out at a gym, going to a tanning salon, etc.

34. Your mate makes excuses to walk to the corner store. He or she could be using the pay telephone in the store to set up a secret rendezvous.

35. Your mate welcomes the weekends or evenings when your children from a previous relationship visit. This gives him or her the freedom to cheat while you are looking after the kids. (Note: A remarried man saw his children from his first marriage every other weekend. The second wife would arrange to attend social functions, nightclubs or go out with her girlfriends only on the weekends when he had his visitation. Coincidence? No. She was cheating and eventually got caught.)

36. Your mate mentions a friend, neighbor, co-worker, course instructor or classmate more often than usual. Comparisons are being made! (Note: When two people are together and one person has more confidence than the other, it sometimes makes the less confident person feel insecure. When this happens, the insecure individual may seek out somebody, usually of the opposite sex, in which to confide. He or she often will begin comparing you and this new confidante just before beginning an affair with him/her.)

37. Your mate goes to bingo games or some other social activity but never seems to spend or gain any money. This can apply to both sexes, but more likely to women cheaters, because generally in affairs the man spends the money.

38. Your mate always volunteers, perhaps insists, upon driving the baby-sitter home.

39. Your mate takes *an unusually long time* driving the baby-sitter home.

40. Your mate frequently cuts short social engagements or dates with you for no clear reasons.

41. Your mate frequently cancels dates or engagements with you using lame excuses.

42. Your mate doesn't take you to public functions or social events and avoids having you meet her new friends. This may apply to occasions that are work-related, sports-related or just leisure-time activities.

43. Your mate makes excuses about why his or her wedding ring is not being worn. "Oh, I forgot to put it back on after I painted the room" or "I forgot to put it back on after I put on hand cream" are common responses.

44. Your mate stays at a friend's home every time he or she goes out for a night on the town. Sometimes your mate "just has to get away" and doesn't return until much later…like the next morning!

45. Your mate attends a social event with you and continually speaks with one particular person of the opposite sex, especially towards the end of the evening.

46. Your mate and you attend a social gathering and she ducks away and disappears for minutes at a time. It may be a hasty meeting with someone else or an opportunity to use the telephone to set up a rendezvous with a lover.

47. Your mate makes excuses to get out of a social commitment or family gathering on holidays that he knows you will have to attend. He may be doing this to spend time with a lover.

48. Your mate claims to spend a good deal of time at the local mall but never buys anything.

49. Your mate has a night when she regularly attends a social function such as a poker game, bingo, crafts session or hockey game. This is a routine spouses and significant others become accustomed to. If your mate is cheating on one of those specially reserved nights, she will always go out, even if the event has been cancelled or the paramour can't make it, just to keep up appearances at home.

50. Your mate says his wedding ring is lost. Make sure there's a good reason why he took it off in the first place.

51. Your mate attends a regular social or business event, sports match, night class or volunteers at some organization, but is always late coming home. He or she might be going elsewhere after the event or not attending it at all. (Note: I was attending a professional course that met in the evening. All the people taking the course would go to a nearby bar after class once or twice a week. One particular young woman would stay for thirty or forty minutes, then leave. We all thought she was going home to her husband. Instead, we later learned, she was meeting her lover. She apparently had been telling her husband she was always late because she was with us. I discovered she'd been having this affair for quite some time, but had no intention of leaving her husband. When the course was over, she told her husband the course continued for another month. She kept up the routine no matter what happened. If, for example, her lover couldn't meet her, she would still disappear for a few hours until it was time to go home. The husband never found out and, to the best of my knowledge, they're still married.)

52. Your mate doesn't return your call promptly when you call on his/her cell phone or pager. If this happens infrequently, don't be alarmed, but if it occurs often then it may be something to watch closely.

53. Your mate is working at the computer and when you walk into the room, he quickly exits whatever program is running, turns the computer screen down, turns off the monitor or clears the screen so you can't see what was there. Your partner probably was on a chat line or reading E-mail that you are not supposed to see.

54. Your mate's vehicle smells of gas, liquid wrench, WD-40 or any other industrial type of odor after a night out on the town. (Note: This may sound strange, but one cheater spilled gasoline in the trunk of his car to douse the aroma of perfume that permeated his vehicle. Another cheater sprayed liquid wrench onto a strap and placed it on the back seat floor area to mask the smell of his lover.)

55. Your mate moves the furniture around in his or her residence often, particularly leaving an open space near the windows. (Note: One victim of cheating arrived home to find the plants from the window ledge placed on the kitchen table and the bench that always sat in front of the window moved elsewhere. Luckily for him, a neighbor saw a strange man leaving the house through the kitchen window. His unfaithful mate's friend had kept guard at the window, playing lookout.)

56. Your mate begins doing the laundry, a chore he or she never used to do or starts doing laundry at odd times for no particular reason, when previously he or she had set days or times to wash clothes.

57. Your mate frequently washes the clothes he or she has been wearing that day immediately upon arriving home. Both this sign and Sign #56 may demonstrate that he or she is trying to

remove the scent of smoke or perfume or the stains of makeup or bodily fluids.

58. Your mate and you own or rent a vacation cottage or camping site, but your mate says she can't spend the whole weekend there with you. She may arrive late on Saturday, saying "I had to work" or "I wasn't feeling well." If this occurs frequently, it could mean she is taking the opportunity to "play" at home while you are away.

59. Your mate often goes to your weekend or holiday get-away place (or a friend's or relative's house) without you, especially during weekdays when he or she knows you can't be there. (Note: A male bus driver who worked split-shifts would drive from 7 A.M. until 9 A.M., then wait for a call from his best friend, who would tell him when the friend's summer cottage was "safe" for him to use. The bus driver would then get in touch with his lover and take her to the cottage. They would have sex and then go their separate ways. The man would attend his afternoon shift, driving from 1 P.M. until 4 P.M. and his wife, who worked days at a local hospital, was none the wiser.)

60. Your mate convinces you that taking separate vacations is a good thing for you both. Perhaps this is true, but this also is a perfect opportunity for him or her to be meeting a person from a computer chatroom or a local lover.

61. Your mate hides a bottle of deodorizer or other odor removal product in the bedroom, under the bed or in the trunk of his/her car. These may be used to remove odors that could be suspicious. (Note: A man who worked in the construction trade and had to travel to the building site would be away

from home all week and then travel four or more hours to be with his fiancée on the weekends. He discovered a bottle of Febreze under the bed, which first puzzled him and then made him suspicious. He confided in me and I recommended that he invest in a Tele Monitor 2000 (you'll learn more about this device later in the book) so he could learn just what was going on in his girlfriend's bedroom. He did this and now they are no longer engaged. It turns out she was having an affair with another woman while he was away and would spray the mattress before putting on fresh sheets.)

62. Your mate frequently tells white lies—mostly about errands supposedly taken care of—which you continually discover to be untrue.

63. Your mate has unusually strong opinions or reactions to illicit affairs and unfaithful partners as portrayed in the media (news stories, movie scenes, reality programs on television, etc.). He or she is either overly critical or overly tolerant.

64. Your mate comes home with grass stains on the rear end or the knees of his or her pants. I would guess it's pretty safe to say golf was not the activity of the day. You should also look out for beach sand in her shoes or other clothing when there is no reason for it.

65. Your mate often has dirt and mud smears on his or her car (from driving down and parking on little-used dirt or gravel roads). (Note: One cheater told me that she and her lover would park her car on a deserted dirt road and make love. Then she would have to go wash her car off.) I suggest that if your mate begins washing his car often, especially late at night, you may have reason to be suspicious.

66. Your mate suddenly begins going into work or exercising at the gym very early in the morning. (Note: I've caught two cheaters (male and female) both of whom told their partners they had to get to work at earlier times than usual, but who, in reality, were meeting lovers.)

67. Your mate angrily says you don't have the right to know what he is doing every minute of the day or that you are trying to control him, after you ask an innocent, seemingly innocuous question about his whereabouts or schedule for the day.

A Personal Note

I find this embarrassing to recount, however I feel it is important to do so particularly here because it has to do with what is discussed in Sign 67: *control*. Despite the facts that I get paid to spy on people, I get paid to notice things other people don't even see and I get paid to unmask cheaters, when it happened to me, I didn't even see it coming.

The worst, most hurtful relationship in which I was ever involved was with an girlfriend who cheated on me. And she didn't have just one affair while we were together, she had many. I'll call her Madeleine, although that is not her name.

Madeleine had transferred to a new job during the course of our relationship and worked on a construction site surrounded by some 3000 men. My work schedule as an investigator was not the normal nine-to-five so when Madeleine went out while I was working, I would always ask her where she would be in the event I wanted to get in touch with her or perhaps meet her somewhere later for a drink or a meal.

When I did this, Madeleine would become angry and tell me that I was trying to *control her*. In truth, all I wanted to know was where she would be so I could contact her, not check up on who she was with or what she was doing. I trusted her. Of course, as I wrote this book and actually listed the signs and signals of a cheating mate, I quickly realized how many applied to Madeleine.

Having a very moody nature, Madeleine would cause arguments over the littlest things. I came to feel that I had to "walk on eggshells" whenever I was around her.

Finally, I discovered just a small portion of her betrayal and ended the relationship. To my shock and disbelief, she begged and pleaded with me to come back, denying most of what I knew to be true. At that time, I told her that somebody would tell me the whole truth someday. Since then, I've found out a good deal more about her cheating ways than she thought I would ever know.

In my experience, as time goes by, the cheater's family members, friends and acquaintances who seemed unsympathetic to your plight with the adulterous mate (or perhaps refused to believe cheating was going on), eventually come to understand both sides of the story. They begin to see what is the truth and what is a lie, what parts of the story are reasonable and what parts don't make sense. In my situation, my ex-girlfriend would tell her friends, family and lovers stories that made me look bad, and then she would say the exact opposite when she was with me. Many of these people told me about these stories later. Despite my sadness, I decided that if she had cheated that much, ending the relationship was the best thing I could do.

After a while, Madeleine began leaving notes, cards, food and flowers on my car and at the front door of my house. She left messages on my answering machine. She sent virtual greeting cards via E-mail. She even used her child as a pawn sending a note in the youngster's handwriting that read, *"We really miss you. We want you back!"* I felt sad at this manipulation for I had come to love the child like my own.

Despite my telling her our breakup was permanent,

Madeleine continued to send love notes and cards and sometimes show up at my door or knock at my bedroom window in the wee hours of the morning. Once I even woke up in the middle of the night startled to see her standing at the foot of my bed.

Months after it was over between us, she said to me that she knew how deeply she had hurt me and our relationship but hoped she could still make it right.

Looking back and trying to understand the relationship I had with her, I realize that Madeleine constantly was manipulating me with her changing moods and by telling me I was always try-ing to control her along with other statements she made. She was trying to keep me off-center and unbalanced. At the time, though, before I figured out just what Madeleine was doing to me, I was really distraught. Besides losing sleep, I lost twenty-eight pounds in the course of our relationship breakup.

I credit three of my best friends with saving my sanity. My closest friend and his wife saw the emotional ups and downs I was going through after the breakup. Trying to help me, my friend told me that if I ever went back to Madeleine, he would end our friendship. I certainly valued his friendship more than the disastrous relationship that was bringing me nothing but pain and emotional upheaval. I chose my friend...and a fresh start.

Later I met a girl who listened and understood where I was coming from because she had gone through something similar. I had known her for years, but never really talked to her one-on-one. It turned out that we shared a great deal and we came to know each other more intimately on an emotional level. We became best friends and, over time, we became so close that our affection for each other turned into a close and wonderful physi-cal and emotional relationship. And I thank God everyday for her, our families and my friends.

I reveal my personal experience with a cheating mate in these pages, because I want you to understand that such a situation can happen to anyone. Don't feel stupid. Don't feel naïve. Don't feel that you should have seen it coming. I'm a professional in this arena and I didn't. Another "don't," however, is don't be caught flat-footed. Read on to learn more signs of a cheating mate.

THE EMOTIONAL SIGNS

1. Your mate is more attentive to your needs than usual. This is due to the guilt feelings experienced by the cheater in the early stages of his or her affair. The attention will diminish as the affair continues.

2. Your mate begins buying you gifts—lots of gifts. These are *"Guilt Gifts"* purchased because your partner feels guilty about betraying you and showering you with presents makes him or her feel better.

3. Your mate's behavior is causing a gut feeling in you that something isn't right. If this happens, pay attention to your instincts. Ignoring them means you want to blind yourself to the truth. You know your mate's habits, routines and attitudes better than anybody, so be suspicious when these things change.

4. Your mate frequently picks fights with you. Doing this gives him a reason to get mad and storm out of the house and thus the opportunity to meet a lover. A cheater may also do this because of the mixed emotions he is feeling about betraying you.

5. Your mate constantly talks about your relationship ending when you fight or argue. She says things like, "What would you do if our relationship ended?" or " If anything ever happened to us, I would always love you like a friend." In general, she seems very negative about your relationship. Your

mate makes these statements, because she has a lover to fall back on if your relationship ends. If your partner repeats these kinds of statements often, be suspicious.

6. Your mate becomes very *moody*. He or she seems very upbeat and excited when leaving you but acts somber and depressed when around you. If your mate is in a long-term affair, he/she will try to keep both relationships running smoothly. Any problems the cheater has in one relationship will spill over into the other relationship as well. This is inevitable.

7. Your mate never talks to you. You live together but don't interact. He has become cold and inconsiderate of your feelings.

8. Your mate's taste in music suddenly changes. For instance, she always listened to pop music but suddenly starts listening to country music. Your partner might be listening to and growing fond of this new type of music because her lover listens to it.

9. Your mate lacks self-esteem. This doesn't necessarily mean he will go out and have an affair, but an insecure individual often looks to others for guidance. If an insecure person's needs aren't being met, he might find the desired feelings of security and positive feedback in an affair with someone else.

10. Your mate continually criticizes another person. She is trying to make you think that type of individual would never be of interest to her, although there actually exists a secret attraction.

11. Your mate criticizes things about you that he or she once found attractive and appealing.

12. Your mate easily becomes offended at the comments, how-ever harmless, that you make.

13. Your mate stops paying attention to you, your children and home-life in general.

14. Your mate begins closing doors when you are around, when before he or she would leave them open. For instance, the Bathroom-Door Rule: Couples in long-term relationships often leave their bathroom doors open while attending to necessities even if their partners are nearby. As affairs develop, the cheating mates will close bathroom doors, dis-tancing themselves physically and psychologically from their partners.

15. Your mate stops complimenting you on your looks.

16. Your mate stops saying, *"I love you."*

17. Your mate acts guilty when you do something nice for him or her. You are supposed to be the person who is making life miserable and the relationship untenable. By doing some-thing nice, you force the cheater to think about what he or she is doing.

18. Your mate turns the table and accuses you of cheating but has no evidence.

19. Your mate would rather spend time with friends than be with you.

20. Your mate shows no interest in your relationship's future.

21. Your mate stops being affectionate.

22. Your mate is more interested in reading a book or watching television than talking with you or making love to you.

23. Your mate frequently talks about the problems a friend, neighbor, co-worker, course instructor or classmate of the opposite sex is having.

24. Your mate begins using new catch phrases or starts to tell types of jokes or express opinions that are unusual for him or her.

25. Your mate pays less and less attention to your children. They seem to sense something is wrong and don't seem to be as emotionally healthy or secure as they once were.

26. Your mate has been acting emotionally distant and withdrawn but when you ask about it, he doesn't want to discuss it and becomes very protective of his privacy.

27. Your mate seems disinterested and distracted during sex.

28. Your mate talks in her sleep and mentions the name of a particular person on more than one occasion.

29. Your mate seems startled or confused when awakened. This uncertainty may be caused by not being sure which bedroom and which lover's bed he or she is in.

30. Your mate's behavior is such that your friends begin asking you what's wrong. Close friends and family members often will notice tension or discord between the two of you before you are fully aware of it.

31. Your mate easily becomes offended when you make normal

and natural inquiries and may demand to know why you are checking up on him or her.

32. Your mate's sleeping pattern changes considerably from the norm and may include unexplainable exhaustion, restlessness, frequent nightmares and sleep-talking.

THE PHYSICAL EVIDENCE

1. Your mate's car's passenger seat frequently is moved to a different position when you get in.

2. Your mate's supply of tissues or napkins in her vehicle is being used up rapidly.

3. Your mate suddenly stocks his car with packages of moist towelettes.

4. Your mate has unexplained stains (passenger or rear seat) in her car.

5. Your mate suddenly buys and installs seat covers for his car. This is especially suspicious after he has spent a night out on the town or a weekend trip away from home.

6. Your mate usually cleans his or her car on the weekend but gets the interior cleaned by a car-cleaning establishment after a night out of the town. A popular excuse: "My friend drank too much and was sick in the car. I had to get it professionally cleaned."

7. Your mate's clothing sports makeup stains or unfamiliar hairs of different color or length.

8. Your mate's car, bedroom, bathroom or hairbrush may contain unfamiliar hairs.

9. Your mate's car windows show signs of excessive condensation. Condensation shows up as little dots on the glass and builds up on the windows if people are parked for lengthy periods. There also may be streaks on the glass if the condensation was wiped off with bare hands or napkins.

10. Your mate's car has little notes drawn in the window condensation, such as a heart with an arrow through it or the words "I love you."

11. Your mate's car displays unfamiliar footprints anywhere inside. If lovemaking occurred during foul weather, interior parts of the car (e.g. backseat) or floor mats may be wet in places that wouldn't normally become wet from ordinary use of the vehicle.

12. Your mate's car contains unfamiliar jewelry (watch, earring, necklace, brooch or pin).

13. Your mate's car contains condoms.

14. Your mate carries a change of clothes in the trunk of his or her car.

15. Your mate carries grooming products (shampoo, deodorant, towel, cologne, soap, perfume, hair dryer, or brush and comb) in his or her car or brings them along when going out for an evening of socializing with friends.

16. Your mate's vehicle is missing the passenger-seat cover, particularly the bottom half.

17. Your mate's car is suddenly missing all of its seat covers. If there was a stain on one, it's easier for your mate to remove them all than explain why one is missing.

18. Your mate lives in an apartment building with a designated parking space for her car. You visit unexpectedly and discover your mate's car is parked on the street and another car is parked in your mate's parking space. It can happen occasionally, of course, that someone parks in the wrong spot, but if you find it occurring repeatedly, write the license plate number down and investigate further.

19. Your mate's car contains parts of flowers, gift-wrapping paper or ribbons.

20. Your mate says he is taking a business trip but few or no kilometers or miles are put on the car.

21. Your mate's gasoline purchases are inconsistent with the kilometers or miles put on the car. Your mate might say the car is suddenly gobbling up huge amounts of gas, when in truth the money is being spent on cheating activities.

22. Your mate's vehicle frequently has the aroma of an unfamiliar smell, such as perfume, cologne, cigarettes or cigars.

23. Your mate doesn't smoke, but there are cigarettes or ashes in the car. Watch for burns in the upholstery also. If he or she does smoke, look for unfamiliar brands showing up.

24. Your mate has scraps of paper or matchbooks with telephone numbers or notes scribbled on them littering his/her car or tucked away discreetly in the glove compartment.

25. Your mate's long distance and/or calling card charges increase dramatically. Your bill will show the numbers called, so call them and ask some questions.

26. Your mate is constantly checking the detailed billing on your cellular telephone to see who you've called. This can benefit you in two ways.

(A) Detailed billing works to catch a cheater who uses a cellular telephone to call his or her lover. Keep notes or a daily log when your mate leaves you. Compare the dates and times of departure, as he or she will usually call a lover very shortly thereafter. Check for the most frequently called number(s).

(B) Detailed billing also reassures the insecure cheating mate that you are not cheating on him/her. The unfaithful partner will check any frequently called numbers that appear on your statement.

27. Your mate, if cheating, will usually use any free time to communicate with his or her lover. If you are suspicious, press *69 (to get the phone number of the last person who called) or press redial on the telephone without being seen, then leave your partner's place for a short time to run an errand or some other excuse. When you return, press redial again to check out the last number. If it's a new, unknown telephone number, check it out.

28. Your mate takes a last-minute trip out of town or says he/she just needs some time alone. This gives a cheater plenty of time to be alone with a lover. He or she can check into a hotel at leisure, knowing that you will not be trying to contact your mate. (Note: One man called his mate and told her he had to go out of town on a last-minute business trip. By coincidence, his wife was driving to pick up a surprise present for him

when she spotted his vehicle parked at the rear of a local motel off the highway. She knocked on each door until he answered. The scene was not pleasant.)

29. Your mate calls you while on a business trip and says she has to stay one extra day but can't stay at the hotel she has been in because it's overbooked. If your mate says this, be wary. Most motels and hotels will often let a patron stay an extra day without asking him or her to leave; hotels usually keep a few rooms available to allow for this kind of occurrence. (Note: One partner, Jeffrey, suspected his mate, Kara, was having an affair. He even had the name of the man with whom he thought she was having the affair. Kara told Jeffrey that she needed some time to herself. She needed to go away for a long weekend alone, which she did. Jeffrey decided to investigate on his own. Two days after Kara returned home from her getaway weekend, he called the hotel where she stayed. He pretended to be the man whom he suspected was his wife's lover. Using the suspected lover's name, he told the hotel that he couldn't find his receipt for the date he stayed there, and he gave them, of course, the date his wife had stayed there. Jeffrey told the desk clerk he would appreciate it if the clerk would fax him a copy of the bill to be used for his income tax. The clerk did and Kara was caught!)

30. Your mate begins to work extra hours (and doesn't seem to mind). This could be an excuse to have extra time with a lover. Check your mate's pay stubs for overtime pay. If there is none, then question her.

31. Your mate won't give you the keys to his or her house or apartment, even though he has yours. This is a type of

manipulation that gives your significant other the freedom to do what he wants yet still have control over you.

32. Your mate spends hours visiting computer chatrooms or reading the personals section of classified ads or e-mailing people you don't know. Be concerned if he/she stays up late at night or gets up in the wee hours of the morning to sign onto the Internet. If you are not on a set fee for online access, check for any large costs or the hours logged on your telephone or cable bill for your Internet access use.

33. Your mate takes her engagement and/or wedding ring off when sunbathing or tanning. Cheaters do this to eliminate tan lines left by the ring. Cheaters then take off the ring(s) and place them in a pocket or purse when out for a night on the town. (Note: I was in a local coffee shop one night shortly after the clubs had closed. A semi-drunken fellow struck up a conversation with me. He pulled his wedding band from his pants pocket and remarked as he put the ring back on his tan, unlined finger, "I better put this back on before I lose it or Momma will be really mad and wonder why.")

34. Your mate comes home to you and is not wearing the same clothes he or she had on when leaving the house. A common excuse is that a person was sick or spilled a drink on his/her clothes so a friend offered replacement clothing.

35. Your mate comes home and you notice certain pieces of his clothing missing. This could be a sweater, shirt, underwear, nylons, socks, etc.

36. Your mate arrives home and takes a shower or bath right away, even if you want to make love. This also applies if an

individual begins taking showers upon arrival home from work, which is something he or she never did before. Most people won't make love to a second person until they've cleaned themselves up first.

37. Your mate's underwear or lingerie is missing from his or her chest of drawers or is discovered in the dirty clothes basket.

38. Your mate refuses to make love to you when you stop by his/her place unexpectedly. No clear reason is given. Do not force the issue. Instead, check around for clues in the closet, back hall or porch. The lover may still be there hiding. Check the wastebasket in the bathroom for condom wrappers and check for a towel left under the bed. A car leaving quickly might also be heard. Be alert. (Note: Daniel told me he once visited a woman and had sex with her. Unexpectedly, her boyfriend arrived home, so Daniel hid in the closet. He over-heard the conversation between the two of them. The boyfriend had been drinking and tried to convince her to make love to him. She made up excuses and finally the boyfriend fell asleep in the bed next to the closet. Daniel left the apartment without being caught. The woman later mar-ried the boyfriend and they now have a child.)

39. Your mate comes home and says he/she has lost jewelry such as a watch, earrings, a necklace, a bracelet, etc.

40. Your mate arrives home and has an unfamiliar pungent smell or taste on his/her hands or genitals.

41. Your mate's genitals or hands smell like rubber from wearing or using a condom. Sometimes he/she smells like chocolate, honey, strawberries or some other food commonly considered

an aphrodisiac or used in lovemaking. Condoms also come in different flavors!

42. Your mate arrives home late and sleeps somewhere other than your bed. In the morning, he or she may say, "I didn't want to disturb you when I got home." What has been left unsaid is that your mate didn't want to take a shower or bath and arouse any suspicions but also didn't want you to smell anything suspicious on his or her body. The cheater will almost always immediately take a shower or bath once he or she wakes up.

43. Your mate, a male, hides his naked body (usually his upper torso) from you. He may be hiding scratches on his back.

44. Your mate, a female, hides her naked body from you. She may be hiding bruising or red marks on her inner thighs, breasts or buttocks.

45. Your mate returns home and his/her clothing is wrinkled, on backward or disheveled in some way.

46. Your mate's collar, sleeve, shirt or jacket is marred by a smudge of lipstick.

47. Your mate arrives home and there is a tan or pink color substance on his jacket or sleeves. This may be smudged make-up or foundation.

48. Your mate's clothing smells of cigarettes, perfume or after-shave and he or she doesn't have a reasonable explanation.

49. Your mate can't maintain his erection. If this is a frequent

problem, without any medical or other reasons (drug use, alcoholism, work-related stress, etc.), beware.

50. Your mate ejaculates only a small amount even though it's been a long time since you last made love. Be aware of the masturbation excuse. (Note: A woman who was cheating on her mate was very paranoid that he was cheating as well. After they made love, she would go into the bathroom and see how much of a deposit he made in her on toilet paper. He wasn't cheating, but eventually she was caught. They have worked things out and are still together.)

51. Your mate's genitals are well lubricated even though she's been out drinking. Most women need some type of outside lubrication to help lovemaking especially if they've been drinking heavily, because the alcohol in their system retains the water in their bodies. Think about previous times when you wanted to make love to her after she'd been drinking. Did it take more than the usual foreplay to get her turned on? Did she need lubricant? If she comes home tipsy and needs nothing, you should be curious.

52. Your mate is wearing a different deodorant, cologne or perfume than what he or she normally wears. It might even be different from what was worn earlier that day.

53. Your mate's sexual desires or lovemaking style changes. Research has shown that when people cheat, their sexual appetites for their faithful partners increase at first but then diminish as their affairs continue.

54. Your mate's underwear, pants or pantyhose have secretion stains, hard and crusty spots or an unusual cologne or perfume

smell on them. (Note: A woman once told me she found her husband's hard, crusty underwear under their couch and discovered pubic hairs on it that were a different color than hers. A hidden camera was set up in the living room and revealed his affair with the next-door neighbor.)

55. Your mate comes home and is not wearing any underwear, even though he or she was wearing it before going out. Cheaters sometimes use their underwear to clean themselves up and either throw the underwear away, hide it or take it off with the intention of putting it in the wash later, but then they forget about it.

56. Your mate's car contains underwear, nylons, socks, a shirt or some other clothing hidden, rolled up or stuffed under the seat or in the glove compartment. Either the cheater or the lover has taken off the garments and forgotten them.

57. Your mate's breath has the smell of alcohol on it even though he doesn't drink. This could be because he was kissing someone who was drinking. Or you've noticed a change in your partner's drinking habits.

58. Your mate wears new jewelry but has no receipts for it. Some excuses she might use include: buying the item(s) from a friend, at a yard sale or flea market or that the jewelry was a gift from an employer for a job well done.

59. Your mate begins wearing sexy underwear such as thongs, high-cut panties, silk underwear and boxers when normally he or she wouldn't wear such things even if you requested it. If your partner says he/she got them at a sale too good to pass up, then check for receipts or a bank withdrawal slip for the

date, time, amount and store where purchased. Receipts tell a story and indicate the patterns of your mate. If there is no receipt, then the items might have been given by his or her lover. Be especially wary if you and your mate are on a tight budget.

60. Your mate starts to wear a new variety of colognes, perfumes, hair spray, gel or make-up.

61. Your mate secretly rents a post office box or rents one openly but refuses to give you a key or let you receive your mail there. (Note: Cheaters rent post office boxes to communicate with people they've met on out-of-town business trips or the Internet. This creates more distance between themselves and their spouses or partners that will help them when they decide to leave their original relationships permanently. Watch out for new bank accounts as well.)

62. Your mate's income tax return contains expenses for unexplained travel or business trips that you know nothing about.

63. Your mate keeps condoms in his/her purse or wallet even though the two of you don't use condoms. Some cheaters will say they were holding them for friends and forgot to give them back.

64. Your mate inadvertently leaves a paper trail and you discover unexplained receipts for hotels, motels, clothing, meals or jewelry, gentleman's or woman's clubs (business cards, matches, marked napkins or coaster's from strip clubs, etc.) Credit card receipts may be in your mate's wallet, purse, clothing or car. Monthly bank or credit card statements will reveal a partner's cheating ways, too. (Note: One cheating

woman would shop after her husband had left for work in the morning then hide the items she'd bought in the trunk of her car. When her husband came home at night, she would tell him she was going out to do some shopping. Instead, she would meet her lover. Later, she would return home with the items she'd bought earlier that morning. This is an example of why you should check receipts for *where* and *when* items were purchased. (I remember once, my ex-girlfriend—yes, the same one—brought home a calculator that flipped up to allow it to stand on an angle from one end. I had seen it at her apartment and thought it was really stylish and unusual. It bore the logo for a rental company on the top. I asked her if I could have it and though she was very reluctant to give it to me, she finally did. It wasn't a paper trail, however, it was a clue for me that I never picked up on. Turns out, she was sleeping with the guy from the rental company who gave it to her.)

65. Your mate refuses to allow you to use the family credit cards or see the monthly statement.

66. Your mate is maxing out all your credit card accounts. Sometimes this is in preparation for ending the relationship with you.

67. Your mate has hidden—and you discover—a love letter or note from another person in his or her clothing, car or E-mail.

68. Your mate opens a new bank account or says you both need separate accounts. (Note: This is a good sign your mate may be preparing to end the relationship. He or she might be hiding money in order to be financially prepared for the break-up.)

69. Your mate begins receiving his or her personal mail at work. By doing this, the paper trail (detailed cellular telephone billing and credit card statements) is hidden from you.

70. Your mate begins changing and washing the bed linen every-day even though that was never the usual routine.

71. Your female mate begins receiving a male visitor at home. You can discover this fairly easily, especially in a household consisting of females only or one in which sons are at school most of the day. I speak of the toilet-seat test. If you are male and arrive home and the toilet seat has been left in the raised position quite often, that is a sign that a man has visited your home. Women never leave the toilet seat up.

72. Your mate's jacket, wallet, purse or car contains unsigned notes or telephone numbers on pieces of paper, matchbook covers, cigarette packs or cocktail napkins. Most telephone numbers a cheating mate writes down or has won't have a name next to them. If they do, it will be a first name or initials only.

73. Your mate goes out for a night on the town and arrives home looking and smelling better than he or she did when leaving the house. Cheaters usually shower or bathe shortly after they've had sex. If they said they were going to local pubs or nightclubs, they should smell like cigarette smoke or beer when they get home, not soap, body spray, deodorant, cologne, perfume or shampoo. (Note: If a woman takes a shower or bath, she will most likely lift her hair up off her shoulders, therefore the back of her neck or bottom of her hair may be wet. A man will more likely take a shower and may wash his hair with a different shampoo. A woman may douse herself in fresh body wash or spray.

If you suspect your mate, check all the places that fresh deodorant soap would linger longest—armpits, back of the knees, back of the arms or triceps, back of the neck, body hair, chest and stomach. You may want to check the inside of your mate's clothing if you can't pick up the scent on his body. Check his waistband, underwear and shirt neck.

A woman will freshen her make-up and spray on fresh perfume, while a man will check his hair and might touch up with some new or different cologne that he keeps in his car. He will often be chewing gum or sucking on a mint. Think about this: When was the last time you went out with your mate and he/she freshened up on the way home?)

74. Your mate may stop and pick up something to eat or drink on the way home as an excuse for his or her late arrival. If your partner is later than stopping for food should allow or if it happens quite often, be wary.

75. Your mate makes frequent unexplained or unjustified automatic teller withdrawals from your bank account. This could be a sign of a gambling problem or a sign that an unfaithful partner is using the money to court a lover. A gambler often will make two or more withdrawals in a short time frame whereas a cheating mate usually will not.

76. Your mate unknowingly has a used condom lodged in his underwear or between her legs, which you discover while engaged in foreplay. (Note: This seems like a far-fetched story, but it happens. A cheating woman used a condom when she was with her lover but never used one with her mate. One night she had sex with her lover and the condom came off but was never found. Later she was intimate with her mate and he pulled the condom out from between her legs. Needless to say, she had some explaining to do!)

77. Your mate (female) seems to be using tampons at irregular times. (Note: One of my clients kept discovering his mate's tampons in the wastebaskets during times other than her periods. He thought nothing of it at the time, but we eventually discovered she was having an affair with someone at work and using the tampons to soak up excess fluids.

    A similar story involved a women who supposedly went out for a night with her girlfriends and arrived home wearing a tampon. Her mate discovered it and knew she was not having her period. She later admitted to him she was having an affair and used the tampon to soak up her lover's semen.)

78. Your mate has, in unusual places, the facial sparkles or hair glitter that women and entertainers sometimes wear at parties and bars. If your partner's clothing has sparkles on it, this may be the result of only a hug or a slow dance. However, if your mate has sparkles underneath clothing or on the skin, you might be right to be suspicious. Check also for sparkles and glitter inside your mate's vehicle.

79. Your mate has an extra toothbrush at his or her place or, if you live together, your toothbrush is missing or shows signs of having been used by someone else. You might also notice a spare toothbrush or its wrapper in a wastepaper basket.

80. Your mate and his/her lover are flushing away used condoms and you discover them clogging your pipes or in your septic system even though you and your partner never use them. (Note: Clyde, who works for a sewage treatment business, told me about a strange experience he had while draining a septic system in a rural neighborhood. The farmer who owned the property asked why the system wasn't working properly and Clyde told him there were a lot of condoms in

the tank and it was hard draining the system. In fact, they were one of the reasons the system was backed up. The farmer got red in the face and stormed into the house. Clyde said he could hear the farmer arguing with someone—presumably the farmer's wife. Later, he saw her throw a suitcase into a car and drive away from the house.)

81. Your mate is selling or transferring the ownership of many family goods, properties and assets (presumably to prevent them from becoming part of the property settlement in a divorce). If your partner begins to sell heirlooms or other items without a justifiable reason, then be suspicious and be aware there may be somebody else in his or her life.

I discovered a story on the BBC News, which reported that Japanese wives are turning to forensic science to catch their cheating mates. Apparently, there is a private detective agency with offices in Osaka and Tokyo (the company president is Takeshi Makino) selling off-the-shelf forensic kits to women called "S-Check." The kits contain two aerosol cans of chemicals that, when sprayed on clothing such as underwear, highlight any traces of semen.

The first chemical is sprayed on your mate's underwear and then the second. If there are traces of seminal fluid, the stain turns bright green. The test relies on the fact that semen is released from the urinary tract for up to two hours after ejaculation.

The company also sells an "Infidelity Detection Cream" which is rubbed onto your mates back before he or she goes to work. A blister will form if the individual showers or bathes between leaving for work and arriving home. Rubbed into socks, it will change the color of the fabric if the socks are taken off for longer than fifteen minutes.

You may feel that using such products is going too far in try-ing to discover if your mate is cheating. If he or she is not unfaith-ful and your suspicions are unfounded, your mate's discovery of your use of such tactics could cause the relationship to founder.

Your knowledge of my 180 telltale signs of cheating, however, is something you needn't share with anyone, particularly your mate. Simply know the signs, be aware of your mate's behavior and begin to take action if he or she exhibits some of the signs. Take time to think about the signs and reasons that lead you to believe your mate is cheating. Write them down on the list which follows. Use additional paper if necessary. Remember: If your mate consistently displays six or more of these signs, it would be wise to look further into his or her activities. In the next chapter, I'll show you how to do it.

Reasons Why My Mate Might Cheat

1._____

_____

2._____

_____

3._____

_____

4. _____

_____

5. _____

_____

6. _____

_____

7. _____

_____

8. _____

_____

9. _____

_____

10. _____

_____

Some thoughts from Dr. Weiner:

Now you know the signs. They are numerous and have always been so, but you may have been unable to see them. Change was occurring, but you barely noticed. This is most likely to happen when the partner, male or female, without conscious awareness, becomes a collaborator. The kind of person who is very needy, dependent and willing to settle for the crumbs instead of a full-blown, equal and mature relationship is the type who falls into the "no see, no hear, no smell, no touch, no taste" category. If that is you or strikes a bell somewhere, it is now time to open your eyes and not only smell the roses but also pull out the weeds. You do this through action, whether it be leaving your mate, seeking counseling, confronting him/her or reaching for forgiveness. If you opt for the latter, it can be done only if a wandering mate pledges true fidelity. Not just with words but with actions. This only happens when the remorse is genuine and not spinning off the top of his/her head to appease you at the moment. Usually, without counseling of some type, this is not very likely to happen. Yet, it is a possibility.

The key here is that something needs to be done and it is you who must do it. It will have far-reaching effects. Not only in this, your marital/relationship situation but in all others as well. For if you wore blinders here, chances are you did so in other circumstances as well. Making a change, becoming aware of new insights will lead you out of the fog. If, in this process, you need professional help, get it. You owe it to yourself. Living with doubt, fear and the powerlessness that betrayal brings is not living life as it should be. Read on and your blinders will fall off and drop into the dust where they belong.

❖

chapter five

❖

Surveillance and Investigation Tips

Surveillance is a very serious and potentially dangerous endeavor. Ideally, you should hire an experienced, licensed professional to perform this type of undertaking. A governing body or licensing commission licenses private investigators who must follow certain rules and guidelines. If you are ignorant or unaware of the guidelines, you could get yourself into difficulties. Be aware that there is a thin line between following a subject and stalking. Thus, in good conscience and as a professional, I must recommend that you *not* perform surveillance, because you and whoever is with you could be seriously hurt or find yourselves in legal troubles.

However, if you can't afford a private investigator and have noticed the signs of a cheating mate, then this chapter will help you learn how to follow and investigate a subject.

First of all, you must be very disciplined and prepared for what you might see and learn. Sometimes the shock of actually having your suspicions confirmed can be disorienting.

Of the three couples whose stories we have been following throughout the book, only Dave surveilled his cheating mate. Of course, he stumbled upon her parked car at Steve's house purely by accident, but then he parked down the street away from her car and waited for something to happen. When Steve pulled into his driveway, Dave immediately was there demanding answers. That is how he discovered the truth about Mary's infidelity. He didn't plan to do it, but Dave used surveillance to find out what he needed to know.

Liam hired a private investigator to perform surveillance on his wife Wendy. However, Liam took it upon himself to do some preliminary investigating and he purchased equipment which allowed him to record Wendy's telephone conversations. These recordings proved to him that his wife was indeed cheating on him. Specifics about this type of equipment and how to purchase it are given in the following chapter.

Julie, too, did not tail her mate, but she did her own form of investigating by calling the phone number she found in Ben's pocket and manipulating his secretary into allowing her to pick up mail Ben was having delivered to a post office box so she could check his telephone and credit card billing statements. Unfortunately, she also found herself reading love letters sent to him from his out-of-town mistresses. It hurt, but ultimately Julie was happy that she took matters into her own hands and became proactive rather than reactive. In the same way, surveillance and investigation of a mate suspected of cheating may give you peace of mind or may confirm your worst suspicions. Either way, you will have knowledge, power and the ability to act.

Naturally, the goal of surveillance is to obtain as much information about the subject as is necessary *without* getting caught. You must understand that if you are going to perform surveillance it may take more than one try or one day to catch a cheating mate. *Preparation is vital!* Remember the Boy Scout motto: "Be Prepared."

There are two types of surveillance—**stationary surveillance** and **mobile surveillance**.

Stationary surveillance can be broken down into three sub-categories:

1. Surveillance from a parked or immobile vehicle
2. Surveillance from an office building, apartment, hotel/motel room, etc.
3. Surveillance using camouflage, which usually consists of utilizing several different vehicles, hiding places or disguises.

Camouflage surveillance often is used by the A.T.F. (Alcohol/Tobacco/Firearms) officers, customs and excise officers and drug enforcement officers. It is also used by private investigators to spot cheating mates and insurance disability frauds.

Mobile surveillance can be broken down into two sub-categories:

1. Surveillance of a moving vehicle in a moving vehicle
2. Surveillance of a subject on foot

The truth about any covert surveillance is that it is really *boring*. As a private investigator once said, "It's fifteen hours of patience for fifteen seconds of panic!"

If you plan to carry out surveillance on your mate, you have to be conscious of the fact that he or she will spot *you* faster than anyone else who comes into view. It would be wise to try to change your appearance a bit, whether you do this through clothing, hair, hats or other disguises.

You will need *vehicle surveillance* for both **stationary surveillance** and **mobile surveillance**, *foot surveillance* in case your subject(s) walks into a mall or gets out of his/her vehicle and *camouflage surveillance* to watch from a location not suitable for a vehicle.

To perform surveillance on your suspected cheater, please follow the simple rules and suggestions I list here. Take time to prepare and acquire the necessary items.

Surveillance Tips

- Use a vehicle other than your own—either a rental car or a vehicle owned by a friend with which your mate isn't familiar. (Note: If you wish to keep what you are doing a secret, then switching vehicles with a friend or coworker may make *them* suspicious of *you*. This will be your time to concoct a plausible story as to why you need to borrow his or her car so often.)

- Pay in cash if you rent a car or use a friend's credit card and pay him or her back in cash. A cheating mate might check your credit card statements for suspicious charges because he or she is afraid you're cheating as well. Therefore, never use your own credit cards.

- Switch vehicles, whether rented or borrowed, as much as possible. This may be difficult for you to manage, but a professional private investigator will switch vehicles as many times as needed to prevent the subject from suspecting he or she is being followed.

- Use a car that is dark in color and dirty on the outside. A clean, shiny, waxed vehicle will bring more attention to you than a dirty one.

- Wear clothing that matches the color of the car's interior and keep both sunshades down. This makes it difficult for the subject to see into the interior of your car through his or her rearview mirror.

- Drive a vehicle with tinted windows. Even if only the rear windows are tinted, you can hide yourself in the rear seat during stationary surveillance.

- Keep a supply of street maps with you. You should have some knowledge of the area you're watching. In most cases, you won't know with whom your mate is cheating or where he or she lives, so you'll just have to follow your mate to discover the location. You don't want to get lost!

- Take a couple of jackets, sweaters or sweat shirts that match the color of the interior of your vehicle and a couple of different hats to wear in case you must get out of your car and follow the subject on foot. If you have a wig, bring it along. I know an undercover police officer that used a hat that had a wig with a ponytail sewn right into it. It was very convenient!

- Park your vehicle, on a sunny day, in a way that the sun shines into the rear seat but not into the front (unless you plan to get in the back seat). If the sun shines on you, you will be easy to spot, as well as uncomfortably hot. Park next to a hedge, under a tree or any other shaded location.

- Lock the car doors—always! If you are spotted, the subject might try to sneak up on you.

- Prevent your automobile's daytime running lights from coming on when you turn the key. To remedy this on most vehicles, put the emergency brake on slightly just before you start the vehicle. The lights will not come on. On the downside, your emergency brakes will be on slightly until your brake shoes wear down a bit.

- Remove the front license plate from the vehicle you are using (if legal in your area). Even if the subject recognizes your vehicle, he or she won't be able to confirm those suspicions if the license plate can't be seen.

- Disconnect or unplug one of the front headlights to give the impression a different vehicle is behind the subject when surveilling at night. Some private investigators equip their vehicles with a switch that can turn one headlight or the other off. (Note: The only problem with the previous two tactics is that local police may pull you over for a spot check.)

- Pull the fuse or disconnect the interior (dome) light of the vehicle you are using. You may have to remove the bulb from its socket. This way it won't turn on every time the front door is opened and be visible when surveillance is occurring at night.

- Turn your car's engine off when parked. If you are parking at night in a rural area, try not to let your vehicle idle because the engine noise will travel quite a distance. Also, engine exhaust is a dead giveaway anywhere.

- Lose any false sense of security you may have as a result of wearing sunglasses when watching your subject during the day. People who wear sunglasses when doing surveillance sometimes make the mistake of thinking, because their eyes are darkened, the subject cannot see or recognize them.

- Utilize your rearview mirrors when stationary surveillance is being done.

+ Do not smoke. A lit cigarette will give away any person(s) seated in a vehicle, especially at night. A pile of cigarette butts on the ground outside the front car door is another dead giveaway.

+ Switch sometimes from sitting in the driver's seat while doing stationary surveillance to sitting in the passenger seat. Pretend you are reading a newspaper or a book to give the impression you are waiting for the driver to come back to the vehicle.

+ Raise the hood of the car if you don't have to stay in an area for long. This gives the impression the car has broken down or overheated and needs a few minutes to cool down.

+ Purchase an electrical inverter, a useful piece of equipment often used by private investigators that may be found at your local sporting goods or electronic equipment stores. It's like having an electrical outlet in your car. Inverters come in 50-watt, 150-watt and 250-watt units. It plugs into your cigarette lighter, which gives you power to plug in your battery charger for a video camera if needed. Don't forget to check your local second-hand shops for inverters to save money.

+ Use your inverter in the cold winter months when you plan to sit in one area for a lengthy period of time. A low-voltage heater can be plugged into it, keeping the inside of the vehicle warm. This way the vehicle emits no exhaust and appears to be abandoned.

- Empty your bladder and fill your gas tank if you plan on surveilling your subject for a long period of time. There's nothing worse than needing to use the lavatory or discovering your vehicle's fuel is low when you are stationary and can't leave the area for fear of losing your subject.

- Top off your fuel supply and use the lavatory quickly when your subject stops during moving surveillance. Take the opportunity whenever you can, because you can't stop for anything if your subject isn't stopping.

- Be prepared to use the great outdoors as a lavatory if necessary. Have a roll of toilet paper with you. Men might want to take an empty bottle with them. This allows you to empty your bladder without getting out of your vehicle.

- Take some food along in case you get hungry. In addition to calming your nerves, chewing gum also helps keep you awake if you plan on being in one location for a while.

- Be aware that if you are parked in a rural area, you will be noticed more quickly than in other places. In small towns where everybody knows everybody, people are more likely to stop and ask if you need any help or just drive by your vehicle slowly to see what's going on.

- Purchase magnetic signs with a bogus company name on it for the doors of your vehicle. These signs are not costly and will give you the appearance of attending to company business. When people see these signs on the sides of your vehicle, they are more likely to dismiss any suspicious thoughts they may have as to why you are lingering in an area.

- Do not park directly under a streetlight when surveilling at night. Rather, search for an area so dark that your vehicle can barely be seen at all.

- Keep coins for pay phones readily available if you don't have a cellular phone. If you do have a cell phone, you might still need coins in case you drive out of your phone's service area. The pay phone money will come in handy if you need to contact a friend to help you or if you've hired a baby-sitter and want to check in with him or her.

- Keep coins handy for road tolls, too. You don't want to be slowed down and lose your subject because you have to get in a long toll line and wait for change.

- Use two or three vehicles simultaneously for mobile surveillance, if possible. This means, of course, that you will have to involve others in your investigation. It's up to you whether or not you want to confide in friends or family members about your suspicions, but be aware that if it's only you performing the surveillance, you're more likely to lose your subject.

- Don't continually drive by the place where you think your subject might be. If you don't attract his or her attention, then you may attract someone else's attention in the neighborhood. Be patient! Your subject will have to leave the premises sooner or later.

- Ask friends or neighbors, as casually as possible, where they've seen your mate lately. You might have to make up some sort of cover story. I suggest you not talk to any of your mate's close friends, as they will probably tell him or her of your inquiries.

◆ Be as open as you can with friends and relatives who are loyal to you. I've learned that the more people who know of your suspicions about your mate's cheating, the more likely it is that one of them will tell you the truth. Of course, many people won't get involved, because they're afraid it will come back to haunt them. However, those who have your best interests at heart will usually tell you whatever they know that might be helpful. They won't want you to be hurt any further.

VEHICLE SURVEILLANCE

If your heart is set on learning the truth and catching your cheating mate, the things you have on your side are *time* and *opportunity*. You will have access to your mate's private papers and can do a search through their personal items for any clues to their activities. The more information you have, the easier surveillance will be. Of course, *skill* comes into play but a little *luck* helps as well.

◆ Perform surveillance with someone of the opposite sex, if possible. Should others see you, they'll think you're lovers talking. Also, a second person might see things you miss.

◆ Use the second person doing surveillance with you to follow your subject when he or she goes into a building while you stay in the vehicle. If your subject hops on a bus, your surveillance partner can get on the bus while you follow behind. (Note: I once followed a cheating mate who drove her car to an automobile dealership and borrowed another car from the owner. She then drove to a shopping mall, left the car there and got a lift with two people in a truck. She then was dropped off on the street, walked around the corner and down the street where she was picked up by a taxi. She was driven to another vehicle that was waiting in the driveway of a business that was closed.

I took photographs of the female entering her lover's residence as they walked arm in arm, kissing along the way. I sat all night watching the building until the next morning when she got a lift back to the shopping mall parking lot where the borrowed vehicle was parked.

She drove the car back to the dealership and picked up her own vehicle. I followed her back to her house where I saw her kiss her husband as she entered the front door. She was supposed to have been working all night. They are now divorced.)

- Find the best vantage point from which to watch for your subject, one where you cannot be seen. Use binoculars. The further away you sit or park your car while you wait for your subject to get into his or her vehicle, the better it is for you.

- Keep one or two vehicles between your car and your subject's car as you are driving. I can't stress enough that the goal to any surveillance is to remain undetected while still keeping your subject in sight. It helps if you have a good knowledge of the area.

- Slow your vehicle and drop back a bit as you follow your subject on a highway, but stay aware of when the exits are coming up. Get a little closer each time your subject nears an exit so you are ready to take that exit also if necessary.

- Keep at least one vehicle between you and your subject while driving in the city.

- Remember that unexpected turns, pedestrians, other vehicles, Sunday drivers, accidents, breakdowns, traffic jams, fear of getting caught and loss of nerve can all cause you to lose the subject you're tailing.

- Take a road that runs parallel to the one your subject is on if you have a pretty good idea of where she is going. It's easy to lose your subject on city streets and you may have to resort to taking an educated guess as to where she is headed.

- Drop back more if you notice your subject looking in the rear view or side view mirror. He may be on to the fact that someone is following. It doesn't necessarily mean you've been spotted, but you must put more space between the two of you if you want to continue to perform surveillance.

- Stop surveillance activities for a while if you feel you've been detected or your subject is becoming suspicious.

- Keep a good distance between you and your subject if the area you're in is rural, but be wary of the road's unfamiliar twists and turns.

- Increase your speed at every corner then drop back as you catch sight of your subject's vehicle in rural areas. Due to the lack of heavy traffic, it's not as possible to blend in unobtrusively. Be careful not to get too close, but keep in mind that he or she may turn into a driveway or side road if there is a break in your vision.

- Throw your subject off the track if you feel he has noticed someone following him but not detected that it is you. Here are some methods you can use: Change drivers if you have a partner; slump down in your seat; put on a cap or other hat; change sweaters, jackets or shirts. If you have a partner with you in the front seat who is visible, have him hide in the back seat or crouch down out of sight in the front.

- Use a mannequin to make it look as though there were a third person in the back seat. Use a blow-up doll, if you have access to one, or a large stuffed animal and keep it lying in the back until it's necessary to prop it up.

- If your subject pulls over to check if she is being followed, drive past and continue tailing her later. Your best course of action is to pull over further up the street and watch what your subject does in your side or rearview mirror. A corner store or parking lot would work well as a place to pull in, but don't count on one being where you need it. Watch closely in case your subject does a U-turn and heads back in the opposite direction. This is tricky, so use your binoculars if necessary.

- Drop your surveillance partner off further up the street, if your subject pulls over, and have your partner look around and watch. Turn the corner in your car and cruise around the block. If your subject makes a U-turn, your tailing partner can signal you to pick him or her up and together you can continue the tail.

- Wait it out if your subject turns left at a red light and you are caught in traffic. Hopefully, you will be able to pick him or her up again. Possibly, you could turn right and make a U-turn, trying, of course, not to be too noticeable.

- Don't follow your subject if she drives up a one-way street. Look for a parallel street that you can drive along until the one-way street ends and you can pick her up again.

- If your subject's vehicle doesn't come out of the one-way street, park your car and walk carefully (or have your surveillance partner walk) down the street. Your subject may have stopped at an address on this street and that is why you can't pick him up again in the car.

- Don't follow your subject into a parking lot unless it's enormous. Use common sense. The smaller the parking lot, the more likely it is you should wait. If it's a parking garage, then you may have to park on the street and walk in. A surveillance partner could walk in for you while you find a place to park.

- Place a piece of duct tape or reflective tape over a portion of the passenger taillight of your subject's vehicle. (Keep in mind that breaking the light is illegal.) This will help you keep the car in sight at night, although you run the risk of your subject discovering and removing the tape.

- Assume you've been spotted if your subject speeds through a yellow light or runs red light and stop the surveillance for now.

- Be aware that your subject may have pulled over if you lose sight of him after rounding a corner. Drive a little distance beyond where you think he or she might have stopped and try to find a vantage point from which you can watch through binoculars and try to pick up the trail again.

◆ Find a parallel street when you're following your subject in an area where there are a large number of intersections with traffic lights. That way, if you fall one set of traffic lights behind your subject, you can get on the parallel street and try to get ahead of her. Once you see your subject overtake you, immediately return to the original street and continue your surveillance. but be careful, this is tricky. Traffic lights change at unpredictable times.

◆ Remain calm if you see a person of the opposite sex seated next to your mate. Be aware that the person with your mate may also be cheating. Thus, both cheaters may be nervously looking for any suspicious vehicles.

◆ Try to ascertain if the location to which you have followed them is a regular meeting place for them.

◆ Be wary while performing surveillance. If you don't know the person with whom your mate is cheating, you must consider the possibility that he or she might be driving nearby—even behind you—as you tail your cheating mate. If this happens, your mate's lover may become suspicious and not go to the rendezvous point, whereupon your cheating mate will call him or her to see what went wrong. Your mate's lover will then describe what you look like and you'll have been caught.

◆ Be observant if your mate appears to be waiting for someone. Do not watch him so intently that you don't notice his lover approaching. That's a good way to get caught. Be aware of your surroundings when sitting or stopped.

• Don't get frustrated if you lose sight of your subject on your first try. It happens to the best of us. First-rate surveillance requires no less than three cars with radio communication. If you haven't been caught, consider yourself a good investigator and continue your surveillance.

• Keep a log of your subject's movements. Chances are he or she will go back to some of the places visited before with a lover.

FOOT SURVEILLANCE

You should know the area well when conducting foot surveillance. Be aware of taxis, trains, subways, carriage rides, motels, hotels, restaurants, movie theatres, back alleys, malls, paths through woods, etc. In order to catch a cheating mate, you have to out-think, be one step ahead and basically put yourself in his or her shoes.

Foot surveillance is much more difficult than vehicle surveillance, because there is a greater chance of being spotted. You should try to find out all the names and addresses of your mate's best friends, close relatives and hangouts in case you lose him or her while performing foot surveillance. This way, you might be able to pick up the trail again by checking out these locations.

Your appearance is also a factor. Dress to suit the occasion. You cannot wear shorts into a fine dining restaurant or a suit and tie to the beach. Common sense should dictate what you wear. You may lose track of your subject when you leave to get the proper attire, but chances are good you will be able to pick up the trail again later.

• Don't stand out in a crowd. However, a person who is taller or shorter than average may do just that. If you're as tall as a professional basketball player, then foot surveillance could be difficult for you.

◆ Carry plenty of cash and credit cards with you while doing foot surveillance. You never know what may come up. Coins might be needed for pay telephone calls or public transportation if you must leave your car behind.

◆ Use places for surveillance where your mate would have to look closely to pick you out of the crowd. If you're in a building looking outside, then stay back from the windows. I was taught in street-survival courses that if I was a sniper waiting for the signal to take out an individual, I shouldn't let the barrel of the rifle hang out the window, giving my position away. Instead, I was to sit back and not let anybody know where I was.

◆ Consider that a dimly-lit bar with a view of your subject who is outside may seem advantageous, but you must keep in mind the possibility that he or she will walk inside.

◆ Don't enter a restaurant or bar that your subject and his or her lover are in unless you want a confrontation. They'll probably see you as soon as you pass through the entrance. In a smaller establishment, you will be noticed right away, whereas in a larger one, you might get away with hiding somewhere out of sight. Use a back door or kitchen entrance only if necessary.

◆ Keep in mind your cheating mate will probably sit with his back against the wall to keep the entrance in view.

◆ Do not make eye contact with your subject. If she is looking around a lot, then hide, look away or turn your back.

Step into a telephone booth or mingle at a bus stop with a crowd of people. Reflective glass or a window will help you keep an eye on your subject while you have your back turned.

- Tape a small mirror to a notebook or a long metal instrument (similar to the kind a dentist uses to look at your teeth or about the same size). This will allow you to stand or crouch down by a corner or entryway and hold the mirror out to see what is going on in another room or down the street. I have completed numerous street survival courses where I was taught to do this. This is a commonly used device on television shows and though it may seem a bit over the top, it really works.

- Stay outside if your subject enters a building with a lot of exits. You'll have a hard time keeping track of her and you're better off outside. Your subject may have entered the building for the purpose of losing anyone following her or your subject may walk straight through the building to catch a taxi or bus. Also, her lover may be on the other side of the building waiting in a vehicle.

- Park your vehicle further away than normal and walk to the building your subject has entered in rural or non-city areas. You must work harder and smarter in such areas to avoid suspicion.

- *Do not* storm into a place where your mate and his lover are and *do not* confront them when you see them together. Discovering the truth of a mate's infidelity can be very stressful. Negative emotions will start bubbling to the surface and you'll want to either leave before they come out or rush in and have it out with him. Please resist these impulses.

* Record the building's address and the license plates of the vehicles parked in the driveway of the location to which you have tracked your mate and his or her lover. Ask around in the neighborhood to see if anyone knows who owns the cars. In this way, you may discover the lover's identity.

* Listen to your common sense when you discover your mate is meeting someone in a secluded location. What you think is happening, probably is. Most affairs take place in a vehicle, hotel or motel, cottage, summer home, trailer, a friend's residence, a lover's residence or your residence.

Familiarize yourself with the tactics discussed in this chapter by following a friend or co-worker without his or her knowledge. You may try to pick a vehicle out of traffic and follow it. This practice will give you some idea of what to expect before you follow your suspected cheating mate.

Whatever type of surveillance you try, be prepared for the possibility that you will catch your mate cheating. You must be ready for the onslaught of emotions that will surely come. Though you may want to react irrationally you need to maintain your composure. To help you do this, think now about what you would do and how you would feel if you caught your mate cheating. The more you think about this in advance, the more time you have to prepare yourself for a painful scene without an emotional outburst. The calmer you are, the easier it will be to decide what course of action to take next.

If you want to know the whole truth, however, one of the worst things that can happen is being caught performing surveillance by your cheating mate before all your evidence is gathered! Once you're caught you will most likely never have another opportunity to find out the truth about your mate, so BE PATIENT!

Note: You can be confident that the advice I've given is proven and valid. As of this writing, in all my years of performing surveillance and investigating adulterous acts, my cover has never been exposed nor has a subject confronted me.

What follows is a simple surveillance planning chart. Please use it as you start out but feel free to add to it and customize it to your situation as you become more experienced with surveillance.

Surveillance Plans

Place: _____

Date: _____

Time: _____

Bring: _____

Other Info: (suspected lover's name, vehicle description, license

plate number, etc.) _____

Place: _____

Date: _____

Time: _____

Bring: _____

Other Info: _____

Place: _____

Date: _____

Time: _____

Bring: _____

Other Info: _____

Place: _____

Date: _____

Time: _____

Bring: _____

Other Info: _____

Place: _____

Date: _____

Time: _____

Bring: _____

Other Info: _____

Place: _____

Date: _____

Time: _____

Bring: _____

Other Info: _____

❖

chapter six

❖

Tools of the Trade
& Where to Get Them

The equipment needed for surveillance can be expensive. Since your needs are personal not professional, I'll avoid discussing the high-tech gear that the average person usually can't afford or, in most cases, will only use once (hopefully).

One store I use and suggest is Radio Shack for some of these purchases. They have stores throughout North America, which makes their equipment inexpensive and easy to obtain. Other stores might give you a better price or more powerful equipment, but Radio Shack and a good second-hand shop are really all you need.

Electronic repair technicians and telephone personnel, the linesmen or women who install your telephones and telephone lines, are quite knowledgeable about listening devices and surveillance equipment.

There are numerous spy shops throughout North America that will send you a catalogue. There are also many on the Internet. The following list gives some of these companies; However, the information is subject to change as businesses sometimes change names and telephone numbers, go out of business, etc.

Spy Shops

1. Probe, Inc. (Spy Tech Agency)
   8519-8521 W. Sunset Blvd.
   West Hollywood, CA 90969
   U.S.A.
   Tel: (310) 657-6333
   Fax: (310) 657-8714

2. E D E Spy Outlet
   2480 Niagara Falls Blvd.
   Tonawanda, NY 14150
   U.S.A.
   Tel: (716) 695-8660
   Fax: (716) 695-7380

3. Counter * Spy * Shop
   of Mayfair London
   9557 Wilshire Blvd.
   Beverly Hills, CA 90212
   U.S.A
   Tel: (310) 274-7700
   Fax: (310) 274-0212

4. The Spy Store
   9986 N. Newport Highway
   Spokane, WA 99218
   U.S.A.
   Tel: (509) 466-4038
   Tel: (509) 626-5949
   Fax: (509) 466-9705

5. Spy Shops International
   600 W. Oakland Park Blvd.
   Fort Lauderdale, FL 33311
   U.S.A.
   Tel: (954) 563-1779
   Fax: (954) 563-7774

6. Spy Shops International
   Canada
   Tel: (416) 704-5722

Internet Websites

1. Virtual World of Intelligence: Spy shops
   http://www.virtualfreesites.com/covert.spyshops.html

2. Spy shops International Inc.
   http://www.spyshops.com/service.html

BINOCULARS

One thing you will definitely need if you plan to do surveillance of any sort is a pair of binoculars. You can usually borrow a pair if you really need to. Someone you know is bound to have them, perhaps a friend or relative who lives in a rural area or near the water.

If you can't borrow a pair, then search the second hand shops in your area. Sometimes they'll have a relatively inexpensive pair that's still just like new. You might even be able to make a trade to cover the expense.

Obviously, the more powerful the binoculars the better, but sometimes you just have to settle for what you can get for your budget. If you're interested in knowing about the best strength and size, talk to the staff at a photography shop. They'll tell you the power best suited for that bird-watching course you plan on taking (hint, hint).

A pair of 7 X 50 binoculars shouldn't be too expensive and is an ideal strength for what you need. Keep in mind that the smaller the binoculars are, the less noticeable they'll be. If you wear glasses, some binoculars have rubber pads that keep you from scratching your lenses.

WALKIE-TALKIES

If you have a surveillance partner, you may want to use walkie-talkies. Because you'll only need one channel, an inexpensive set will do. Radio Shack carries a model called TRC-91, Catalogue Number (Cat. No.) 21-1614, which has a range of approximately one-quarter mile. Radio Shack also has a mini-size one channel, the TRC-505, Cat. No. 21-409 which weighs only 5 ounces.

The TRC-234, Cat. No. 21-1678, has 3.8 watts of power. This comes with a car adapter and forty channels. Also available is a

TRC-506, Cat. No. 21-406, which is a one channel, voice-activated set for hands-free communication. The transmission range is good for approximately one-quarter mile or 400 meters.

Obviously, the more watts the walkie-talkie has, the larger it's range. Any obstacles such as buildings, hills or mountains might interfere with the transmission.

Remember that people in the area with police scanners will pick up almost anything you say on the walkie-talkies. If you plan to use them, make up a code. Practice it before you actually use the gear. Keep the gear at a friend's place.

Citizen band (C.B.) radios work just as well as walkie-talkies, so long as you have the time for somebody to install it. Radio Shack sells a TRC-501, Cat. No. 21-1701, which is a 40 channel C.B. The problem is you'll have to buy two. If not, you can purchase one and buy a walkie-talkie that's compatible with the C.B. The person with the walkie-talkie can (by using camouflage gear in a tree-covered area) watch the subject's residence while the other person sits down the street in a vehicle waiting for a signal that the subject is on the go. A couple of cell phones work just as well, but the airtime, if it's on peak time, could cost you quite a bit of money.

(Note: Something to keep in mind when using C.B. radios. I was performing stationary surveillance in a small town with a second investigator. We were using codes and talking back and forth on the C.B. radio. The local police arrived and spoke to him. I was a little harder to locate. They informed him that the local residents were overhearing some of our conversation on their television sets.)

CAMERAS

If you want evidence of infidelity and need to get a picture of your cheating mate with his or her lover, this could be a problem—one with no easy solution. A good camera with a zoom lens, plus film and development, can sometimes cost between $1,000.00 and $2,500.00.

Not only is it expensive, you also have to be able to hold a camera pretty steady when a picture is being taken with a zoom lens from a distance and without a tripod. Otherwise, it will be out of focus.

If you can't afford an infrared camera or a zoom lens, you might have to settle for a picture from a standard 35mm insta-matic. This won't give you any close-ups, but it might give you enough detail to show your mate you know what he or she has done. Keep in mind that if you get too close, your mate may see you or hear the clicking of or film advancing in the camera.

Talk to the staff at your local photography store about 35mm cameras. They are less expensive than they were years ago and with new technology making advances everyday, who knows what you'll find. An experienced photography manager will usu-ally know the best and least expensive equipment for your needs. If you purchase a camera from a second-hand shop, make sure you use and develop a roll of film first so you can be sure it works.

SCANNERS

If your mate uses a portable telephone, then a police scanner may prove to be one of your best investments. Scanners usually pick up portable telephone conversations easily. Test your scan-ner by using it in your house or walking around the neighbor-hood. You might have to program the right frequency, but in most cases all you need is a scanner with a trunk-tracking system.

A trunk-tracking system allows you to monitor elusive trunk-ing systems used by businesses and emergency services, such as police and fire departments across North America. These groups change their frequencies often in an attempt to prevent private citizens from listening to their conversations.

One reason this was done was to keep criminals who were

committing a crime from hearing the location of the police. Nowadays, cellular telephones are going digital and from the information I've gathered, scanners don't pick up the frequency. My scanner (which is a 200-channel trunk tracking system) picks up telephone conversations, radio conversations and portable telephone conversations. With it I've been able to pick up police, fire, ambulance, businesses, private and personal communication.

If your mate starts to talk on a portable telephone, turn on the scanner and listen. Push lock on your scanner to keep it on that frequency. This way, the scanner won't jump to other telephone or radio conversations. Write down the frequency if you haven't obtained the code from the information supplied on the portable phone.

Keep in mind that scanners may only pick up one side of the conversation on a portable telephone. Try to get a hand-held scanner for easier handling. If you are in your vehicle, use it with the cigarette lighter adapter.

Some private investigators place a scanner (once the frequency is set) and a voice activated tape recorder together in a watertight plastic bag near the subject's home. This should be done in the early morning hours and retrieved at the end of the day. It's not the most effective way to gather information, but it helps.

TELEPHONES

One of the best methods for catching a cheating mate is the telephone system. As mentioned in previous chapters, detailed billing can give you excellent clues.

If, however, you do not have easy access to your mate's monthly billing, there are two ways to get it. Unfortunately, they are both illegal and I don't suggest you utilize either of them. Nonetheless, I am presenting them here so that you will be aware of such methods.

If you don't live with your mate or even if you do but can't get access to the billing information, call the cellular and/or land line telephone company and tell a representative that John or Joan Smith (your mate) didn't get his or her last monthly statement. Ask the company to send a duplicate and then watch your mate's mail until the statement arrives. (*This is against the law and you should not do it!*)

How can you check your mate's mail everyday without arousing suspicion? Gather all those unwanted weekend sales flyers and get a friend to walk around the neighborhood placing them in people's mailboxes. Have your friend check your significant other's mailbox for the duplicate telephone bill.

Another method is to get a person of the same sex as your partner to call the telephone company and tell them there has been a change of address. Have the duplicate bill sent to the friend or to you. After a month, call and change the address back to the original. You do run the risk of getting caught, however, so I say again: *These methods are against the law and you should not use them.*

If your mate is driving in his or her car and you are doing surveillance, a modified radio scanner can be used to pick up cell phone transmissions. However, the frequency of the cellular telephone may change as the vehicle travels and the cellular towers carrying the transmission change. This makes it difficult, because your scanner may bounce from one channel to another while you follow your mate. You may hear only a small portion of the conversations. Also, newer digital cell phones are difficult to pick up on a scanner, if not impossible.

You should have Caller ID installed on your telephone, even if it's just to try out for a couple of weeks or months. If you think this will make your partner suspicious, then make up a story as to why you feel you need it. For instance, you could say people have been calling and hanging up on you frequently. If you live with your mate, you can get the same results by asking a friend to make frequent hang-up calls from a telephone booth while you and your mate are both home. This will reaffirm your reason for getting Caller ID.

The tape recorder is one of the best tools for catching a cheating mate. You can attach a voice-activated one to your telephone and listen to all his or her conversations. Voice-activated tape recorders are easy to obtain (any electronics store) and easy to use.

(Note: One man told me he suspected his wife was having an affair. He wanted me to tap his telephone, but I told him that was against the law. He went ahead on his own and taped his wife talking to her much younger lover as they were having phone sex. She also told the lover how she was going to run up the bills and drain the family bank accounts.

He hired me after listening to the tapes and I caught the unfaithful spouse in action. The couple is divorced and unfortunately, the emotional scars left behind has meant numerous counseling sessions for the children.

Another tape-recorder story involves a man who suspected his wife of cheating. He bought a voice-activated tape recorder and placed it under the passenger seat of his vehicle.

He captured the intimate conversations of his wife and her lover. She denied the affair. While she knew her husband was intelligent, she didn't think he was devious enough to set up such a stunt. She was shocked and upset when he confronted her with the truth.)

Your recorder can be either battery-operated (AC - Alternating Current) or a plug-in (DC – Direct Current). Be sure, however, that it's voice-activated.

If you plan to use any battery-operated pieces of equipment (recorder or walkie-talkie), make sure the batteries are fresh and new. There is nothing worse than going through all the time and energy to strategically place a voice activated tape recorder or prepare to use another piece of equipment and then discover that your batteries have failed.

Radio Shack has other recording devices as well. The Optimus AC/DC desktop recorder, Cat. No. 14-1115 is a good one but it requires the additional purchase of either a micro telerecorder, Cat. No. 43-8957 or a recording control device, Cat. No. 43-8236.

I recommend a Multi-phone recording control device, Cat. No. 43-1236 that plugs right into the telephone jack and then right into your recorder. This way all the equipment remains hidden from view. If you feel nervous purchasing such equipment, you could simply tell the salesperson that you are trying to catch a person making harassing telephone calls to your home or you could say that your child is making calls to a 1-900 number and you want to catch the youngster.

I use these devices on my own telephones when I need to record an angry call from clients' ex-mates after their court dates. Often, because I'm the one who caught them cheating, they figure I'm the one to blame for the relationship break-up. After all, they have to blame somebody, don't they? Of course, I always tell the irate cheating mates that they're being recorded just in case I feel the filing of harassment charges is required.

If you have any questions about the recording length of the tape, ask the sales representative at the store where you purchase the device or call the manufacturer. Ideally, you want it to record for as long as you're away from the house. The longer the tape, the better. Fortunately, these devices are easily hidden.

To hook up the tape recorder and recording devices, you'll need a telephone jack. This jack should be in a part of the house your mate rarely, if ever, frequents. Test the tape recorder. Make sure it records and operates quietly.

If you should want to install another hidden telephone jack, then connecting the colored wires easily does it. Radio Shack sells a book listed under Installing Telephones, Cat. No. 62-1060, that can help you. You also could call the telephone company (if you can't do it yourself) and have a hidden jack installed in an attic, closet, storage barn, garage or any other part of the residence that your mate would never think to look. There will be a charge on your bill for this extra jack, so make sure that your mate doesn't see the bill.

Once the jack is installed, hook up the recording device and the tape recorder. Be sure that the recorder has a tape in it and is set for voice activation. The recorder starts every time the telephone rings or is picked up and stops when the conversation is over. The sound of the recorder cannot be heard on the telephone line.

One drawback of recording conversations is the possibility you'll hear something very upsetting. When this happens, you'll want to confront your mate right away. ***Don't!***

Instead, make a copy of the incriminating evidence. You'll want at least one extra audiotape with this incriminating evidence. But you'll want even more proof than just that one audiotape. Be patient. Time is on your side. Give him or her every opportunity to talk on the telephone with a lover and let your cheating mate give you all the proof you need. The more your mate talks on the telephone, the more you will learn.

If someone (your cheating mate's lover?) has been making frequent hang-up calls, the tape recorder can come in handy. Listen carefully to each call. There might be background noises that give the caller's identity away. You might be able to deduce the caller's gender, whether they're at work or home and whether or not they have children. Someone in the background might even say the caller's name.

If you suspect your cheating mate is conducting an illicit affair in your own home, you might want to set the voice-activated tape recorder up in a closet and place a microphone under or near the bed. A microphone for a tape recorder is not expensive, however, be aware you may also need an extension for it.

Another unique device for surveillance is the Tele Monitor 2000. This unit is a bugging device that plugs into your telephone jack and allows you to listen discreetly to what is going on inside your house, from any telephone in the world. This works well if you have to leave for a trip out of town or you don't have the time to check or replace video or audiocassette tapes.

You simply place the unit out of sight in a room of the house where you think your mate and a lover might be conducting their affair. The unit's sensitive microphone will pick up even a whisper up to thirty-five feet away. You dial your telephone number and enter a code over the telephone to access the unit. The person in the house will never hear the telephone ring. After five minutes, you will be disconnected and you will have to call back. To extend the time, you need to press a number from your telephone.

This is a completely self-contained unit; no actual telephone is required for its operation. It needs no batteries and is equipped with modular plugs for instant connection to the telephone jacks.

The size of the unit is 3 inches X 5½ inches X 1 inch. It can be purchased from the following company:

Spy World Inc.
311 South Division Street
Carson City, Nevada 89703
U.S.A.
Telephone: 1-310-704-1528
U.S. Residents Only: 1-800-779-4423

The Truth Telephone is a device unlike any other. It integrates three vital tools: a desktop telephone, a professional, covert, electronic lie detector and a micro-cassette conversation recorder. The Truth Phone covertly analyzes a person's voice for sub-audible micro tremors that occur with stress and deception. Instantaneously, the system offers a digital numerical evaluation of the speaker's voice stress level. The Truth Telephone is pricey, but may be the piece of equipment you need.

A Truth Telephone is available from Communication Control Systems (C.C.S.). Their World Headquarters is located at:

360 Madison Avenue, 6th Floor
New York, New York 10017
U.S.A.
Telephone: 1-212-555-3040
Fax: 212-983-1278

Catching a cheating mate with your telephone can be the first step toward the peace of mind for which you're searching. However, check with your local law enforcement to make sure that you are not breaking any laws. Sometimes, a quick check on the Internet may provide case law for your locale regarding situations about telephone tapping or recording. It's important to note that I've never read nor heard of a case where someone has been criminally charged for catching his or her cheating mate with a telephone tap. That's not to say that it hasn't or won't happen.

VIDEO CAMERAS

One area I'm asked about quite frequently is video camera surveillance. I've had numerous requests to hide a camera in a bedroom; However, I always refuse. I believe there must be some sort of moral expectation of privacy.

Let me ask you this: Wouldn't it be enough for you to see your mate and his or her lover entering your home, rather than actually see the images of them having sex in your bedroom? Who wants to have those devastating images play over and over in one's mind? I know I wouldn't!

I refuse to set up a hidden camera in any bedroom, but I have set up a baby-sitter surveillance camera in the living room and, if by chance, a client has ever moved a camera into the bedroom later, it's unknown to me.

Covert camera surveillance can be set up anywhere in your home. All you have to do is buy one or rent one. Depending on the size, model and features, the costs will vary.

One I recommend is a CPH1 Color Pinhole Board Camera, which has a 3.7mm lens, is approximately 30mm (width) X 30mm (height) X 14mm (diameter) with 350 lines of resolution. It may be purchased from:

E D E Spy Outlet
2480 Niagara Falls Boulevard
Tonawanda, NY 14150
U.S.A.
Tel: (716) 695-8660
Fax: (716) 695-7380

Another good camera is the Minicam 2, a black and white camera in an aluminum case measuring 25mm (width) X 25mm (height) X 12mm (diameter). It has an F2.0 lens with 420 lines of resolution. It also can be purchased from EDE Spy Outlet. Both cameras can be easily connected to your VCR.

I suggest you call an alarm or investigation company in your area to inquire if either company provides baby-sitter surveillance cameras. They mostly use cameras to catch employee theft and quite possibly will rent one to you with a deposit. Your deposit will be returned when you return the camera with no damage to it. This is the most inexpensive option.

Ideally, you should get a color camera with sound. Ask the company to set it up in your living room or get instructions on how to set it up yourself. The cameras usually come with a VCR that indicates or displays the time and date. I know personally that video evidence used in court requires these functions to be shown on the screen. What you do with the camera is your business as long as you don't damage it. Use a six- or eight-hour Extended Play (EP) videotape. Of course, the VCR should be hidden and inaudible.

OTHER SURVEILLANCE EQUIPMENT & TECHNIQUES

This is a bit unusual, but if you feel you need to obtain a Night Vision Scope or Infrared Monocular (this is one telescopic lens, whereas a pair of binoculars have two lens or one lens for each eye) for surveillance, the easiest place to get it might be a store that carries hunting equipment or Sears.

I've been asked numerous times about where, when and how to arrange a lie detector test. I suggest you call a private investigator or your local police department for information. Private lie detector tests are available, but they are usually expensive. And then, of course, you must convince your mate to take the test!

A trick often used by private investigators is to enter a building where the subject lives and ask other residents in the building about him or her. As usual, a creative cover story would be helpful. The professional investigator will carry a briefcase or bag with him and place the bag out of sight when he enters a the neighbor's apartment or house. When the investigator departs, he "accidentally" leaves the briefcase or bag behind. A half-hour to forty-five minutes later, the private investigator returns for the briefcase saying he forgot it.

The key is that the briefcase or bag has a small, unobtrusive microphone outside attached to a voice-activated tape recorder inside. A briefcase is best because it can be locked. Although the neighbor may say nothing of importance directly to the investigator, once the investigator departs the individual may say something of interest to someone in the residence or may make a telephone call and talk about the investigator's visit. It's often a long shot, but sometimes it pays off.

Bugging Devices

A bugging device can also be used to catch your mate. They're illegal in many areas, but if you're interested in getting one then contact one of the sources listed in this chapter.

One commonly used household item that can act as a bugging device is a baby monitor. Gail suspected her husband of cheating and noticed that he was going into the basement room where their old baby furniture was stored quite often. One day, Gail poked her head into the storeroom so she could ask him to take a trip to the store, but he wasn't around.

Inspired, she removed the insides out of an old transistor radio and placed the unused baby monitor inside. Next, she put the radio shell inside the nursery furniture storage room, then put the baby monitor receiver in her sewing room. From the second floor of the house, Gail heard her cheating mate discussing rendezvous times with his lover on their portable telephone. He was caught!

Camouflage

The purpose of camouflage equipment is to blend into the surroundings without being spotted by the subject. For outdoor surveillance, most or all of what you'll need can be purchased at fish and game stores, army surplus stores, sporting goods and hunter's shops.

If you're performing surveillance during the summer months and plan to be in a wooded area, be sure to pack some bug repellent. Many people can't stand the sound or nearness of insects even if a bug net protects them. Place some bug repellent not only on any exposed skin but also on the outside of your clothing. Ask a seasoned fisherman, fisherwoman or hunter on the best product to purchase.

If surveillance is going to be performed in the cold, then dress accordingly. Take extra clothing, a sleeping bag and an emergency pack that includes a first aid kit, candles, matches and a pocketknife. Keep them in the trunk of your vehicle. If you want to blend into the snow, go to a hardware store and buy a pair of

white coveralls used by painting contractors. These even come
with a white hood which you can use to hide your head.

The equipment I have suggested is all you *should* need to
catch a cheating mate. However, I can't stress enough to use common sense. You should contact a lawyer or your local authorities
before inadvertently doing anything illegal.

Following is a list to help you decide your surveillance equipment needs and to plan a budget for purchasing these items. If
you can't afford to buy all the equipment you'd like to have, rank
the items you feel you need the most from one to five and purchase the two or three most important items on the list first. Each
time you perform surveillance, you'll get a better idea what items
you really need, and those items you can do without.

Equipment I'll Need for Surveillance

Item: _____

Obtain From: _____

Cost: _____

Item: _____

Obtain From: _____

Cost: _____

Item: _____

Obtain From: _____

Cost: _____

Item: _____

Obtain From: _____

Cost: _____

Item: _____

Obtain From: _____

Item: _____

Obtain From: _____

Cost: _____

Item: _____

Obtain From: _____

Cost: _____

Item: _____

Obtain From: _____

Cost: _____

Item: _____

Obtain From: _____

Cost: _____

chapter seven

❖

Checking on
an Internet Affair

The Internet is the largest collection of interconnected electronic networks in the world. These include corporate, government, university, business and research networks. The World Wide Web (www) is the most popular part of the Internet, probably because you can access specially-formatted documents that support links to other documents and audio and video files.

Modern technology is growing by leaps and bounds and learning how to use a computer is really not that difficult. If you are a computer novice, it can be a bit intimidating at first, but once you proceed you'll wonder why you waited so long in the first place. I suggest you take a night course or just ask a friend who is knowledgeable about computers for assistance.

E-mail is a feature on your personal computer (PC) that allows you to send and receive mail electronically via the Internet. Any person who knows how to operate a computer can access a chat line. Chat lines and E-mail are the newest concepts used by cheating mates for getting to know one another and making plans to meet. The average Internet addict spends eleven hours per day in front of the computer signed onto the Internet, according to a report recently broadcast on A&E.

If a person is in a relationship that isn't meeting his or her emotional needs, he or she might be susceptible to meeting someone on a chat line. The potential cheater will probably check his or her E-mail messages quite often, looking forward to communicating with this newly acquired friend. You may find yourself becoming a distant second.

If you plan to check your mate's E-mail, you'll have to open the Internet Web Browser on your mate's computer. The most commonly used browsers are Microsoft Explorer or Netscape Navigator. Once you open the browser, click on the "mail" button, which is sometimes represented by a graphic icon that looks like a letter, to open the E-mail inbox. Unfortunately, when you read your mate's new E-mail messages, he or she will know, because on most systems, once new E-mail messages are opened, they are no longer displayed as *new unread* messages. So, once you check your mate's E-mail, it will be obvious to him or her that someone has already opened and read his or her E-mail. However, on some computer programs, there is an option that allows you to keep the new mail designation even if the message has already been opened. In that case, your mate will never know you've been snooping.

Of course, you may never be able to read your mate's E-mail messages if his or her E-mail account or entire computer are protected with security passwords. Logical reasoning suggests that if he or she has a password, not shared with you, your mate must be hiding something from you. To break through this security barrier, you must try to come up with your mate's password. Try passwords that are associated with something close to your mate: children's names, pets' names, birth dates, friends, favorite numbers, street names, etc. Enter as many passwords as you can think of as you try to gain access to the computer or its E-mail program. It will not hurt the computer and your mate will never know that you have tried to gain entry to his or her computer.

Once you have found a suspicious E-mail message and want to find out the identity of the sender, there are a couple of different ways of learning to whom the address belongs. First, go to a search engine—a Web site designed to help you find specific information on the Internet. Examples of search engines Web sites include **www.infoseek.com**, **www.excite.com**, **www.bigfoot.com**, **www.yahoo.com** and **www.aol.com**. Most of these sites have a feature that allows you to search for people or E-mail addresses which they may call People Finder, People Search or White Pages. Simply choose the people finder option and enter the suspicious E-mail address in the appropriate field. If the person you are searching for has ever registered for anything on the Internet or shopped on-line, there is a great likelihood that information about him or her is available. If you don't have success on your first attempt, try another search engine and then another (different search engines look for information in different places on the Internet—some of which overlap with other search engines, some of which don't).

Another way to search for Internet email addresses is to purchase a book called *The Internet for Dummies* written by John R. Levine, Carol Baroudi and Margaret Leving Young. This book teaches you how to use the Internet and gives ten ways to find email addresses and other information.

The best ways to catch a cheating mate who uses a computer:
- First, go to this Web site: **http://download.cnet.com**. In the empty *Search* field, type *Spector* to download this program to the computer (make sure you are doing this on your mate's computer!). Spector is a program that automatically and secretly takes hundreds of screen snapshots every hour. It records all applications loaded, all Web sites visited, all chat conversations and all incoming and outgoing e-mail activity. Spector allows you to see exactly what the user was doing on his or her computer and on the Internet.

Screen snapshots can be taken as often as one per second or as infrequently as one every few minutes. You also have the choice of recording in full colour or in 4-bit grayscale. Screenshots can be played back like a video recording, displayed frame-by-frame or exported to a BMP or JPEG file.

To save disk space, an inactivity time-out feature is built into the program to stop recording if the computer is not being used. Access to the program is password protected, preventing the user from disabling it. A ten day trial version is offered and an advertisement-free version can be purchased by calling 1-888-598-2788.

• The second method is to go to this Web site: **http://www.keylogger.com** and download the program called Invisible Keylogger 97. This is a keystroke recorder program that runs invisibly under Windows 95, 97 and 2000. It logs all the keystrokes from a computer keypad to a binary file. Obviously, the more money you pay, the more keystrokes the system will log. This can range anywhere from 500,000 keystrokes up to and beyond 2,000,000.

The binary file can be converted to a readable text file later by running a utility provided with the Invisible Keylogger 97 program. This program is not password protected. The purpose of this program is to provide you with a log of what your mate has typed on his or her computer for later review. The final user assumes all responsibilities associated with the usage of this program.

There is a shareware version (a "light" version of the full program that can be downloaded for free) that is provided if you're thinking about buying it. The shareware version has a 500 keystroke per session limit. You will need to restart the program if you want to record more keystrokes.

Just run *ik.exe* again. Also, the shareware version starts itself after the Windows login and password phase. So Windows login and password will not be recorded.

If you want the full program which records a much great number of keystrokes, you can check prices on the company's Web site or purchase the program from:

Amecisco
2258 43rd Ave.
San Francisco, California
U.S.A. 94116

Or send an E-mail for ordering information to:
sales@amecisco.com

There is another, sometimes unreliable, method for accessing user history on most computers called **cache.** This is called a *QUICK ACCESS TEMPORARY STORAGE FACILITY.* It's on the computer's hard drive. This stores all the information downloaded off the Internet under *INTERNET* or *TEXT FILES.*

The reason it is sometimes unreliable is because your mate may know about *cache.* If so, then he or she can easily delete any *INTERNET FILES* or *TEXT FILES* that are stored on the hard drive after disconnecting from the Internet.

In order to get at these files on older computers you have to access a program called *FILE MANAGER.* Then you click on *MAIN FILE.* Once this is completed, your monitor will be split into two screens.

Search for a program called *cache* in the left column. Once you are on this program, click your mouse on *cache* and this will show files on the right of the monitor. Then click your mouse on any *TEXT FILE* or *INTERNET FILE* on the right side of your monitor.

On Microsoft Windows, click your mouse on *START*. This brings up a column with a list of options. Click on *FIND*, which brings up *FILES and FOLDERS*. Click on *FILES and FOLDERS*. This brings up a pop-up box asking the "Name and Location" required. Under "Name" type in *CACHE* then, under "Look In" click on the down arrow. This brings up the drop down list box.

Here you click on the display for (C:) or Pri_DOS (C:) drive (depending on what type of program you have) which will show under "Look In." Click your mouse on "Find Now" which brings up a list of files if any are to be found. You simply click on the *INTERNET FILE* or *TEXT FILE* you wish to view.

If you click your mouse on a file and a pop-up box is displayed showing "Open With" then you have clicked on the wrong file. In order to open this file, you have to know what type of file it is.

For other computer surveillance equipment or devices, visit the following Web sites:

www.spyequipment.com
(1-800-779-4423 - U.S. residents only)
(1-310-704-1528 - International)

www.hidenpeek.com
(Call 1-818-676-0860)

As you gather information about your mate's Internet usage, make sure to write down what you learn so you don't forget. More importantly keep this information hidden so you don't get caught spying by your mate. Use the following page for your records.

My Mate's Internet Info

E-mail Address : _____

Password(s):_____

Frequently Visited Sites: _____

_____

_____

_____

_____

Suspicious Addresses in

Computer Address Book: _____

_____

_____

_____

_____

_____

chapter eight

Making Your Case

Now you've learned why, how and when cheating occurs, the 180 signs of cheating, how to conduct surveillance and investigate your cheating mate in the real world and in cyberspace, as well as which tools you'll need to do the job. The time has arrived to start making your case.

If your investigation has shown that your mate definitely is cheating or is exhibiting too many telltale signs of deception, the first thing you should do is start keeping a diary and a duplicate diary. The duplicate is so that you will still have a record of what you've gathered after you have confronted your mate with the original diary and he or she has ripped it up, thrown it into the flames in the fireplace, driven over it with the car—well, you get the idea. Your duplicate diary should be tucked away somewhere safe and sound.

Keeping the diary is also good for you mentally and emotionally. It keeps you busy and feeling proactive instead of just stewing about your suspicions.

In these daily journals, you'll write down all the information you've collected about your mate's activities, stories, excuses, etc.

This could include a telephone number or business card you discover in a wallet or purse. To avoid arousing suspicion, you might want to photocopy the business card or write the information down and place the card back where you found it.

Keep any cassette or video tapes, pictures, photocopies and other evidence you've uncovered (remember to have duplicates of them, too!) together with the diaries. This will be helpful when the time comes to confront your mate.

The information you record in your diaries must include such details as the exact times your mate leaves and returns from work, overtime worked (supposedly), extracurricular activities, what excuses are given for being late, etc. Having it laid out before him or her gives a cheating mate no way out when you conduct your confrontation. Keep in mind that when you finally make the accusation, your mate will probably accuse *you* of all sorts of misconceptions and generally try to confuse you. Therefore, it's imperative that your journal is accurate and detailed.

Keep your diary for four to six weeks or until you notice patterns developing in your mate's activities, schedule and behavior. Perhaps she seems to work late only on Thursday nights, for example, or he goes to work early every Friday.

If your mate seems to be taking a lot of business trips using his or her car, start writing down the kilometers or miles on the odometer each day. Ask him how the trip went, was it successful, etc., *but don't seem too curious or you'll arouse suspicion.*

Start looking through your mate's personal items. Check bedroom drawers, closets, the bed, mattresses, filing cabinets, the cookie jar, back shed, toolbox, knitting kit, compact disc case, vehicle and even that little tear in the carpet. A cheating mate will go to any lengths to hide an affair.

Change your schedule and notice whether it bothers your mate. By doing this, you may be causing him or her to break secret plans with a lover. This will upset your unfaithful partner. Make note of it in the journals.

Be sure to write down all the discrepancies, large or small, in the stories and excuses your mate relates. If something he or she said just doesn't seem right, casually question your partner's friends and family about his or her recent activities.

EXAMPLE: "Hello, Bill! Did you go out with the boys to watch the game on Sunday night? John drank too much and had to get a lift home. Boy did he have a hard time getting up for work the next morning! Say, you didn't notice if he left his gloves (scarf, sweater, etc.) behind, did you?"

Maybe Bill will offer some information. If not, try one of the other fellows on the team. Be as casual and offhand as possible. You don't want to arouse the friend's suspicion that you are checking up on your mate's activities.

Over time, if your mate has no idea that you suspect cheating is going on, he or she eventually will let his or her guard down and become careless. However, you need to keep the daily log so you can actually see and document his or her behavior changes.

If you discover an unknown telephone number among your mate's things, try calling the number from a pay telephone. Don't speak; just listen to see who answers. It may be the person who keeps calling your home and asking for that wrong number.

If you learn nothing by calling the number, try something else. Most cities or towns have what is called a city directory. This book is used mostly by businesses and is quite expensive. But if you have a friend who is employed by a company that has one and is willing to lend it to you briefly, then you have access to all sorts of information.

The city directory contains addresses, the names of homeowners, adult resident's names, their employers and positions along with other information. It often carries numbers that are unlisted in the phone book. Businesses advertise in it and it is revised each year.

Some information of this type now is available on a CD-ROM instead of book form. You may be able to buy this through a company called Polk City Directories. Check on the Internet or the telephone directory under *Info Tyme CD-ROM* or call 1-800-221-4112.

Here are a few more tips on keeping the diary:

+ Be aware of your mate's various smells. Start smelling his or her clothing and write down these smells in your log, noting the unusual ones. Note the scent of your partner during hugs or when you are close to him or her.

+ Write *everything* down. Do not leave anything to chance.

+ Act like nothing is wrong while still gathering as much evidence as you can.

+ Don't accuse your mate of cheating before all the evidence is gathered. If you do, your mate won't admit it and will be more wary. It then will be twice as difficult to catch him or her.

When you review the diary you are keeping, everything probably will make sense and fall into place if your mate has been truthful. If not, you must decide which parts of his or her actions and stories are true and which are not. This book is designed to help you confront your cheating mate with so much damning information there will be no doubt in your mind and he or she won't be able to explain it away. There'll be no excuses. No newly made up story will be able to exonerate the guilty. Since your gut tells you one thing, common sense tells you another and your emotions impact everything, keeping a detailed log or diary will help you discover the truth.

chapter nine

How to Handle a Lying Mate: Interview and Interrogation Tips

Every person is unique. Every individual does things in his or her own particular way. Lying is no exception!

One form of lying is manipulation—getting someone to think or do as you want him or her to think or behave. Both men and women practice the art of manipulation when they cheat on a spouse or long time partner.

Men usually manipulate with words or gifts. They tell their faithful girlfriends and wives what the women want to hear and frequently buy them presents or "guilt gifts."

Women tend to manipulate with reassuring statements and promises of sex. One of the most common answers given by cheating women to mates who suggest they are unfaithful is, "If I wanted to be with someone else, then why would I be with you?" The implication of this statement being that since she is still with her mate, she must not be seeing anyone else. Obviously, this is not always true.

Men who cheat often give highly detailed excuses once they get home. They might even add some humor. I suppose they assume that the more trivialities and particulars with which they embellish their stories the more believable they will be to their partners. They are worried, of course, their mates will pick up on any parts of the stories that don't sound right. Cheating men always hope there will be few or no questions, but if there are, they'll continue to lie.

On the other hand, women usually will say very little when engaged in cheating. If your wife or girlfriend becomes distant, silent or defensive when you ask her questions, you may have caught her in a lie. When cheating women do offer stories, they are often brief and lacking in detailed information.

Women are afraid their mates will be able to punch holes in long stories. If boyfriends or husbands press their mates for more information, details may be offered but only a little at a time. Cheating women hope that this satisfies their mates and they will stop asking questions.

Sometimes, a woman will make love to her mate in the hope that he'll stop questioning her. Often, his ego will take over. *How could she make love to another man and then make love to me?* he'll think. *No, my mate would never do that. She's not cheating; she loves me too much!*

When a woman chooses not to make love to her suspicious mate, an insecure male may think he upset her with his accusations of infidelity. If he's not 100 percent sure an affair is taking place, he might think, *She may never make love to me again.* He'll stop asking questions.

Go with your gut! Your instinct is usually right. If you suspect your mate is cheating but the evidence doesn't convince you, trust that gut feeling. If you keep a daily log of your mate's activities, you will eventually catch them.

The trick in discerning the truth is in knowing what to watch for in your mate's appearance, tone of voice, behavior and body language. Concentrating on just one characteristic can be deceiving, so look at the whole picture.

When your mate tells you why he or she was out late or gives you some other suspicious story, write it down. Wait a week, then ask your partner about the story again. Listen closely to his or her answers and watch mannerisms and body language. People will always remember the truth, but lies spring from the imagination and people will often forget the details of stories they made up on the spot. Watch for discrepancies in the two retellings of the story.

You must be objective and use common sense as you make an evaluation of your mate's honesty. Two good signs that an individual is lying are a lack of eye contact (the person will often look up as if they're trying to remember) and a pause before the answer.

Watch for these two signs while you're listening to your mate tell you the same story a week apart. If he or she is telling the truth, the story will unfold very naturally and automatically. Remember: The truth is the easiest thing to remember while a lie is something that has to be thought about.

Unfortunately, veteran cheaters already know this and many have mastered the art. They will look you straight in the eye, they don't hesitate to answer and they tell the story just as well the second time. So how do you catch *them*?

Always keep in mind that any story you hear from your mate should be based on common sense and logic. The story either makes sense or it doesn't.

Avinoam Sapir, a polygraph (lie detector) examiner from Israel, says, "Everyone has their own linguistic code. People are pretty consistent with their language choices. Memory works differently than imagination. If a person is reporting something truthfully, it comes from memory. If they are being deceptive, it comes from imagination.

"Look at the differences between memory and imagination. One comes from past tense and one comes from the present. One involves details such as smells, conversations, feelings and the other was built in a vacuum. One has emotion and one does not."

In a nutshell, truthful people and liars answer questions differently. The key is to allow them to provide an *uninterrupted* version of the events.

If a person is fabricating a whole story or bogus event, the Question & Answer technique is helpful *to him or her*. Your questions direct the flow. Information that comes as a result of a question is a less reliable indicator of truth than information that is put forth in an open statement.

Asking questions with snippets of information contained in them can work for you (if you are providing a little bait to catch someone) or against you (if you have included bits that will find their way into a false statement later). Psychics and hypnotists know this best. If they have to rely only upon themselves, it is much more difficult for them to amaze people with their skills. However, if they can talk and interact with their subjects for a little while, they can learn an amazing amount of information which they will then incorporate into their predictions or fortunes.

Analyzing a person's written or verbal version of a story can only work if the statement is a "pure version statement." This means the words belong to the author (your mate) and are not contaminated by an interviewer (you).

Sapir believes the biggest obstacle to getting the truth in an interview is the interviewer. People are more truthful responding to a computer or in filling out a questionnaire, he says.

According to Mamie Murray, a former police officer who is now a polygraph examiner and private investigator from New Brunswick, Canada says 99 percent of people do not lie. They just don't tell the *whole* truth.

People trained in statement analysis learn to look for what is *not* in the statement. Of course, misrepresentation by omission is still a lie.

The polygraph instrument, more commonly referred to as a "lie detector," is a device designed to detect and record physiological functions of the body, such as pulse rate, increases and decreases in blood pressure, respiration rate and changes in sweat gland activity. Changes in physiological functions occur involuntarily as a response to a stressful mental activity—such as lying.

By continuously recording body responses, any changes that occur as a response to questioning can be observed. Under controlled conditions, a polygraphist can evaluate physiological changes and determine if they are consistent with truthfulness or attempted deception.

The accuracy of the polygraph depends upon whether the topic is suitable for testing, the questions are properly formulated and the examiner is competent. When all of these variables are in place, the test has an accuracy rate in the high nineties. If all three conditions are not in place, the polygraph should not be considered as evidence of lying or truthfulness. Such results are simply invalid.

Observing people takes time, but most of us don't take enough time or gather enough information to make a proper evaluation. And, of course, you can't read people accurately if you don't see them objectively.

An example of this type of myopia is the female half of a couple still in the first three months of their relationship—the infatuation stage. The man continues to flirt with every woman he sees, but the woman is so in love she barely notices. She'll see what he's doing eventually, but at that moment her ego and emotions are standing in the way. She lacks objectivity.

Over time and through professional and personal experience, I have come to believe there are certain *types* of deceptive people in this world. I break them down into four categories of prevaricators.

Four Types of Liars:

(1) *Infrequent Liars* tell a lie now and then because they don't want to admit they've done something wrong. It bothers their consciences, but the lies will fit right into place with their well-thought-out stories. In many situations, trusting mates won't know it's a lie they're hearing, because the details can't be easily verified. To catch these liars, listen closely to what they say and carefully examine their body language.

(2) *Frequent Liars* lie more often, obviously. They don't, however, think their lies out as well as infrequent liars do and therefore make mistakes more often. Examine the logic of their stories. You will probably discover it's like Swiss cheese—full of holes!

(3) *Consistent Liars* tell lies so often, even they don't know when they're being truthful or untruthful. Unfortunately, they don't really care, either. The details of the original version of a fictitious story may conflict with subsequent retellings of the lie. Listen carefully. Faithful mates might catch these cheaters contradicting themselves.

(4) *Veteran Liars* tell lies for reasons and plan their deceptions carefully. They have thought the lies through, know exactly what they are going to say and even have back-up plans in case their suspicious mates want to check out their stories. They are very hard to catch. Using common sense, logic and asking many questions will be invaluable in catching this type of liar.

Clues to deceptive behavior and untruthfulness come both in verbal and non-verbal form. According to Detective William (Bill)

Reid, a polygraph examiner in the Saint John Police Force, Saint John, New Brunswick, one must both listen and watch carefully a mate suspected of cheating. If you have been with your mate for a reasonable length of time, then his or her body language should be readable by you when you begin a subtle interrogation. There are some noticeable body language signs that your mate might show if your questions make him or her nervous. Be aware of them.

Body Language Indicating Untruthfulness:

(1) Tapping feet on the floor or drumming fingers on a table or desk.

(2) Touching, covering or in some way shielding eyes from view.

(3) Looking at the floor and not meeting your eyes while offering explanations for his or her behavior.

(4) Blinking his or her eyes excessively.

(5) Talking with hand gestures.

(6) Looking to the left or right, but never at you.

(7) Hesitating before answering, as if to think about the right thing to say.

(8) Flushing of the skin or becoming very pale.

(9) Sweating excessively, particularly on the forehead, palms of the hands and armpits.

(10) Rocking body movements.

Behavioral attitudes also can be used to get a read on an individual's honesty or dishonesty. Once again, strict attention must be paid to determine these attitudes during your interview or gentle interrogation of your mate. It is wise to make notes directly afterward, regarding which of these signs he or she displayed.

Behavioral Attitudes Indicating Truthfulness:

Composed: Truthful subjects usually display composed attitudes. They act and feel in control. Their actions and comments seem reasonable and rational.

Concerned: Truthful subjects normally show interest in the questions they're being asked. They are alert. They will not run away from any questions and often ask some of their own.

Co-operative: Truthful subjects will usually co-operate. They'll do anything to prove their innocence.

Direct & Spontaneous: Truthful subjects are usually direct and quick with their answers. They maintain good eye contact.

Open: Truthful subjects are normally open in speech and posture.

Unyielding: Truthful people generally will not back down when they are wrongly accused. They will constantly interrupt you as they defend themselves. The more the questioner cuts them off, the angrier they'll get. They're forceful and unyielding in their denial of any infidelity.

Sincere: Truthful people will almost always display sincere demeanors. They are sincere and genuine in the things they say and do.

Behavioral Attitudes Indicating Deceptiveness:

Overly Anxious: Deceitful subjects seem out of control. They are very irrational, seem confused, have mental blocks and perform unnatural or exaggerated body movements. They do not appear relaxed and, as the questions progress, their actions and anxious behaviors worsen.

Unconcerned: Deceitful subjects often show "I don't care" attitudes. They try to ignore the problem. Their typical responses are, "Why are you making such a big deal over this?" and "Why are you asking me about this?" They will try to minimize the situation.

Defensive: Deceitful subjects often display unjust anger initially. They come on strong and weaken later. Typical responses are, "Why are you accusing me?" or "My car's broken down before and it's never been an issue."

Evasive: Deceitful subjects are often very non-committal. They won't give a direct answer. Typical responses are: "I don't know. I don't recall" and "Why would I do something like that?"

Accepting/Apologetic: Deceitful subjects often don't become angry when accused of wrongdoing. They accept what is being said. Common responses are: "Can I say one thing..." or "I know what you're saying but..."

Overly Polite: Deceitful subjects frequently come across as insincerely solicitous and cloying. They try to persuade you with kindness.

Complaining: Deceitful subjects will complain a lot. Complaining raises defensive barriers. It avoids the issue and raises unrelated concerns. Typical responses are: "You realize I'm losing pay by sitting here with you, don't you?" and "Why are bothering me? I had nothing to do with it."

Rationalizing: Deceitful subjects will often try to lessen the seriousness of the incident. Example: "All I did was drop off the secretary to her dentist on the way to a meeting."

Guarded: Deceitful subjects are often very cautious with any statement they make. They answer questions very exactly and never volunteer information.

Defeated: Deceitful subjects often seem uninvolved. Their tones of voice are sad and they appear on the brink of tears. If this happens, don't stop. Continue your questions.

Quiet: Deceitful subjects often remain very quiet and still while being questioned. They want to take in everything that is being said. They also fear opening their mouths and somehow giving themselves away.

Behavioral Attitudes that Can Indicate Truthfulness *or* Deceptiveness:

Nervous: Both honest and dishonest people may exhibit nervousness when accused of cheating. This is a normal response. Truthful subjects, however, usually become less nervous once given a chance to defend themselves and refute accusations. Deceitful subjects frequently will grow more nervous as they are questioned.

Fearful: Both truthful and deceitful people accused of cheating by their mates may appear fearful. It's possible they are afraid of being found out regarding other things they've done in the past.

Anger: Both faithful and unfaithful people may show anger at some point while being questioned. With truthful people, anger is not usually displayed at the beginning of the question period, but will increase as the questions continue. Deceitful subjects will often display anger or rage early on in the questioning, trying to bluff their way out of having to respond. Their anger will usually subside as the questions progress and they realize their bluffs didn't work.

When questioning your mate, you need to remain objective and exhibit self-control. This is easier said than done, of course, but you must not let your emotions get the best of you. You don't want to get physical and end up in jail or the hospital. Take the professional advice I give to all my clients: A CHEATING MATE IS NOT WORTH IT!

❖

Conclusion

❖

Thoughts from the Heart

We all have the right to make choices in our professional lives, our personal lives and, of course, our love lives. When you make a poor choice, a choice that is hurtful to others, it's like a black mark on a white wall, obvious and, perhaps, indelible. Although in time, most people will come to forgive you, others may hold a grudge against you for life and never forgive your actions. Unfortunately, mistakes and bad choices happen—they're part of everyone's learning process throughout life.

When your mate cheats, he or she is displaying a low regard for you and a low regard for the value of your relationship. Being in love and entering into a committed relationship with someone means working together as partners and closing the door on temptation.

It is mind-boggling the deceptions people will orchestrate in order to be unfaithful. I've heard so many people say, "If I ever decide to be unfaithful, I will end my committed relationship first. After all, it's the only fair and right thing to do." Well, that sounds good, but do you know how often that happens? About as often as winning the lottery.

Some couples have what are called *open marriages*. It is their understanding that it's okay for each partner to engage in outside sexual relationships. Each partner is allowed lovers on the side without losing the affection and respect of his or her mate. I make no moral judgment about people who choose this lifestyle, but I wonder why they decide to remain married or, even better, why they got married in the first place. Why not remain single?

When a cheater's behavior is revealed, he or she loses the trust and respect that was earned over the course of the relationship. Often, the feelings of remorse are overwhelming for the unfaithful mate. In fact, once caught, the majority of cheaters wish they could go back in time and change what happened. They realize, often too late, what they have destroyed—the trust and faith of their partners, and many times the relationships themselves.

Only when you've been in love so passionately, madly and deeply with your mate and then discover that he or she cheated on you, shattering your expectations and hopes, can you begin to understand the devastating blow of infidelity.

The different partners in the couples we've met in this book have chosen different paths. In Dave and Mary's case, Mary's cheating was supposed to be, in her mind, a one-time fling, not an on-going affair. Although she thought she just needed to be with someone else briefly, her lover persisted. After several meetings, Mary had to admit she had feelings for both her husband and her lover. It was very confusing for Mary, but it was also a relief when the truth came out.

Dave and Mary still live together and both are attending counseling as they try to work out their problems. They continue to work the odd hours and difficult shifts at their places of employment.

Julie and Ben have split up. Ben continues to see his children from his previous marriage and has moved on to a relationship with Julie's friend Betty. Having left her husband for Ben, Betty is struggling to get a commitment from him. Ben indicates he's not interested in that kind of relationship with her.

Julie, trying to move past the pain, is receiving counseling. She has severed her ties with Betty and hasn't dated anyone since her break-up with Ben. She finds she has a difficult time trusting people now.

Liam sued Wendy for divorce, citing evidence of her infidelity. He was awarded custody of the couple's two children. Liam has moved on. He sold his business so he could spend more time with his children and remarried.

Wendy received alimony from Liam for two years so she could obtain training and begin a career. She has periodic, planned visitation with her children. Wendy still denies any responsibility for the break-up of her marriage. She blames the private investigator for causing all the problems. Currently she is dating a man several years her junior. He is not the man who was her lover at the time Liam discovered her cheating.

When my mate cheated on me, I had a choice to take her back or end the relationship. Because her cheating was so egregious and out-of-control, I couldn't handle all the lies, all the deceit. With her, it was one constant mind game after another. In the end, I think (or at least I hope) she realized the mistakes she made, but it was too late for us. I realize now I loved the wrong person too much.

I can only hope that the experiences and emotional pain I've encountered and the stories of Dave and Mary, Julie and Ben as well as Liam and Wendy will help those who are experiencing their mates' cheating behaviors or who suspect their partners of infidelity.

I have learned, through my professional activities and personal experiences, some basic truths that I hope will be of value to you.

My Individual Relationship Values:

- It takes years to build up trust and only seconds to destroy it...

- Instant gratification may give you heartache for the rest of your life...

- You can keep going long after you think you can't...

- Sometimes when I'm angry, I have the right to be angry, but that doesn't give me the right to be cruel...

- Just because someone doesn't love you the way you want him or her to doesn't mean you aren't loved with all the individual has to give...

- Problems can become boulders in your path, that block your way or they can be stepping-stones to a brighter tomorrow. The choice is yours...

- Maturity has more to do with what types of experiences you've had in your life and what you've learned from them than it does with how many birthdays you've celebrated...

- Best friends can do anything or nothing and still have the best time...

- No matter how close your friends are, they may hurt you now and again. You must forgive friends for that...

- Sometimes you have to put the individual ahead of his or her actions...

- Don't be so eager to find out every secret. It could change your life forever...

- Two people can look at the exact same thing or situation and see something totally different...

- There are many ways of falling and staying in **LOVE**...

- Writing as well as talking about things can ease emotional pains...

- Credentials on the wall do not make you a decent human being...

- It's hard to know where to draw the line between not hurting people's feelings and standing up for what you believe...

- Life is what you make it and not what it makes you...

- No matter how hot and steamy a relationship is at first, the passion fades and there better be something else to take its place...

- In relationships, it's easier to blame somebody else for a mistake in judgment than to take responsibility for your own actions...

- Sometimes the people you expect to kick you when you're down will be the ones to help you get back up...

- No matter how badly your heart is broken; the world doesn't stop for your grief...

- Life is too short to be preoccupied with the small stuff...

- Learning to forgive takes practice...

I want to remind all of you who harbor suspicions about your mate's faithfulness and those of you who know that your mate has strayed to listen to your gut instinct and be proactive. Statistics prove that we humans don't have the concept of unwavering love nailed down, but we don't want to give up on the concept either.

Making a decision to continue or end your relationship after your mate has cheated is a very complicated and difficult one. You must consider whether your relationship was worthy to begin with and what it is worth now. You must ask yourself, is a second chance something worth giving my mate? If so, what will prevent him or her from cheating again? Will I ever be able to trust my mate again? If you decide to end the relationship, then make sure you walk away peacefully and silently with your dignity, sanity and pride intact. If you decide to continue the relationship, keep in mind that both you and your mate probably will feel very insecure and unsure of yourselves. Counseling and communication will benefit both of you.

I wish you patience, understanding and lasting love in whatever direction you choose for your life.

Afterword

Some final thoughts from Dr. Weiner:

You have now been given tips for watching for warning signs and surveilling, investigating and interviewing your possibly cheating mate. You have learned that lies and deceptions will be commonplace for those who've cheated. To discriminate and look between the lines, to see the whole picture, you need to maintain a neutral stance. To do this, you have been given, throughout this book, a storehouse of tools. But a tool is only as good as the person utilizing it. A hammer in the hands of someone inept may lead to disaster. The same is true of the implements with which you have been supplied in these pages. The key, therefore, to using your tools most effectively, is YOU. However, if you have been betrayed, you are in an emotional spin. Traumatized, you play and replay the possible scenarios in your mind. Your emotions are a tangled hotbed of fear, jealousy, hurt, frustration, envy, disappointment and consummate rage. Yet, in order to go through with your surveillance plan, to get the facts by being observant, you must stay calm and cool. How can you do this? Here are some tips:

First and foremost, stay focused in the moment. This will stop the clamor of the "what ifs" pecking at your brain. Here is an exercise to help you: Close your eyes and breathe in and out three times. Now picture all of your thoughts as a flock of geese high in the sky. See them in formation together and flying off somewhere, on their pilgrimage to another country, perhaps, another land far away. You have no thoughts on their flight; all you are doing is observing them. You are not attached to them; you are merely a witness to their flight. With this, a new dimension of consciousness has entered. As you release yourself from the urgency, the power which the thoughts have over you lessens, as does your compulsive thinking, your fear. As those thoughts lose their grip on you, a state of peace enters; your stream of *thought-thought-thought* subsides. At first, the gaps of calmness between periods of anxious worrying will be short. After all, you are a newcomer to all of this. But, as you continue practicing this exercise, the gaps will increase. And with them comes stillness and peace.

This sense of peace, this feeling of stillness, brings with it a heightened alertness. For your emotions are no longer pulling you down into the pit where clear thinking is hardly possible. Now you can give all your attention to the present moment. Try this technique in your everyday activities as well. In the bathtub or shower, listen to the sound of the water falling on your body. Feel it. As you move under the flow, listen to your breathing. Pay attention. You have now become aware of a silent but powerful sense of presence. Do this with all of your swirling emotions. Acknowledge them but do not become them. Say to yourself, quietly and with acceptance, *Now I am feeling my anger. But I am not controlled by it.* Don't analyze it. Just watch it.

Once you do that, you can, after a period of practice, sit quietly, in peace, and do the job of investigating, interviewing and learning the truth calmly and with confidence. For only in this becalmed state will you be able to clearly recognize all the signs to which you have been alerted that your mate is not a faithful partner. And, most crucially, you will preserve and protect your own self without becoming debilitated.

The path may be a strenuous one, but now that you have a compass and all the tools you need, including viewing yourself in a new perspective, the end of this winding road is in sight. And LIFE, having presented you with one of its most difficult, painful tests—ascertaining that the person you love may be unfaithful— can once more enfold you in the peace, happiness and joy you most assuredly deserve. Be confident that your new skills will help you recognize and appreciate authentic love when you find it.